HOUSE NAMES
Around the World

HOUSE NAMES
Around the World

JOYCE C. MILES

DAVID & CHARLES
NEWTON ABBOT

ISBN 0 7153 5580 5

Set in 11/13pt Plantin
and printed in Great Britain
by W J Holman Limited Dawlish
for David & Charles (Publishers) Limited
South Devon House Newton Abbot Devon

Contents

CHAPTER 1

Introduction

This book is for everyone who stops now and again to look at the name of a house. So often you pause in astonishment: can people really stoop to such follies, or rise to such heights? The answer, of course, is that they can, and that the extraordinary inscriptions to be seen on the nameplates on some front gates are evidence of a custom which brings delight and satisfaction to a great many people.

So it seems odd that little is known (or at any rate written) about the habit of naming houses. Are names like *Red Roke, Charmaine, Kentricia, Bats Cottage* and *Crumbledown* all symptoms of some strange madness which afflicts suburbanites of the mid-twentieth century?

Is the name of your house the title of your autobiography, or of the chapter you never dared include? And if that is so, what are we to make of names like *Quando, Sally-in-the-Wood, Sans Larmes, Terra Nova, Nuts* and *Doddering Heights?* All these names are actual names of houses and those quoted above all exist.

However unlikely or eccentric some of them may seem, the names given as examples in this book are all real names which people have chosen for their homes, both in the English-speaking world which has been the main subject of this inquiry, and in other countries selected for comparison. The only exceptions are the fictional house names which have long been recognised by authors as an obvious, or subtle means of underlining character and atmosphere. These are briefly discussed in Chapter 10.

Individual identifiable dwellings have existed for quite some time, and this makes it surprising that so basic a habit as the naming of them seems to have aroused so little comment. In the absence of a good many of the usual pointers to investigation it has been necessary to approach the subject in a broad way, looking for recurring patterns in the hope that names will reveal something of the lives and interests of the people who chose them. Some 20,000 house names were collected and listed. Wherever possible this was done on the spot. Historical records and other sources of information produced examples from the past and from remote parts of the world.

The field of inquiry turned out to be wider than had been expected. Naming is far from being a mere device of twentieth-century Anglo-Saxon suburbanites. The custom runs from early history to the present day, from England's Home Counties to Tokyo. Foreign language equivalents of our own familiar names suggest that we share at least some of our domestic attitudes and folklore with other countries, and even with other continents. There is a beautiful ceramic plaque in the wall of a house near Lisbon which says simply *Meu Repouso*—the Portuguese equivalent of that name which to English satirists and cartoonists means the essence of suburbia. The idea of home, a resting place from one's wanderings, is a recurring theme.

Wanderers and travellers have, it appears, carried names around the world with them, and the cross-fertilisation between different parts of the world is quite noticeable. Names have travelled, in particular, between Britain, the United States, and Commonwealth countries. But the process has extended to other parts of the world as well.

And everywhere people display a humour, inventiveness and imagination which deserve more appreciation, and more critical examination, than they seem to have received. There are, inevitably, banalities and disasters, but even these may reveal something of the perpetrator and the society in which he lives. Where the urge to make an effect is so strong, it is only to be expected that the Wee Folk will appear, and that now and again someone will choose a name which already designates some formidable prison.

Most of the roads and streets through which we pass every day are full of this raciness, nostalgia and curious conformity. If the passer-by is led to see and enjoy more of these things, this book will have succeeded in its aim.

CHAPTER 2

Beginnings

Although the practice of numbering houses began in France in 1463 on the Pont Notre Dame in Paris, in Britain it was not until 1765 that a Bill was passed requiring the Court of Common Council to affix street name tablets and to number houses. Some of the bigger cities of the ancient world were probably big enough to make numbering desirable, but in general the landmarks were fewer and changed less frequently, and it was only as late as 1764 that a British invention, the Post Office, began delivering to individual houses outside London. The patterns of movement and communication, and thus of living, which are instinctive to us are comparatively recent in date.

The naming of houses is a much older habit. We know something of the homes and lives of people in the ancient world, and here and there a name has come down to us. It is difficult to establish when man first began to build anything approaching a house, but each year new discoveries are made and new techniques developed which reveal fresh evidence. At one time the oldest known dwelling was thought to be in Zambia, dating from about 55,000BC, but more recent excavations in France show evidence of huts which date back to somewhere about 300,000BC.

In Britain early man is believed to have made use of rock shelters before the last Ice Age, but whether any of these dwellings had a name is something we are unlikely to know. Perhaps they were known by the name of someone who lived there—in which case a simple practice still very much in favour would have a satisfyingly long pedigree.

The caves in which prehistoric man lived 10,000 years or more ago are still immovable objects in the landscape with strikingly distinctive features, and it is reasonable to suppose that our fore-fathers must have named the caves, just as we have in our turn —the Long Hole, the Slitter, Lamb's Lair, Swildon's Hole.

Archaeologists can tell us a good deal about many of the most famous buildings in the ancient world, but in many cases the names by which these buildings have come to be known, even where they have a traditional air, originated in comparatively recent times. In Assyria there was a palace at Babylon called *E Sagila—The House That Lifts The Head*—a noble enough name to set at the head of the list. The Annals of Sennacherib speak of a palace built of ivory, cedar, cypress and spruce 'for my royal abode', and this was known as *Ekal Zag.Du.Nu.Tuk.A— The Palace Without a Rival*.

The civilisation of Rome has left its great monuments all over Europe. Temples and aqueducts, amphitheatres and triumphal arches are visited every summer by thousands of students and sightseers. But in addition to their more famous public buildings the Romans built huge housing blocks for their ordinary people, and fine town houses and villas for their leading citizens.

Many of the ordinary people ate and slept in 'insulae', like the *Insula of Felicula* in Rome. These were blocks of buildings en-closed on all sides by the city streets and therefore called 'islands' (insulae). An insula must have been something of a rabbit-warren, especially after a few years of use and rebuilding. Insulae were usually built and owned by wealthy men and very often bore their owner's name. In this respect Rome and its provincial towns

11

can be seen as forerunners of the custom of naming blocks of flats after a particular person.

The wealthy owner, however, was likely to be found not in the insula that bore his name but in a 'domus'—a large and often magnificent house accommodating only one family. In the city there would be something like one domus to every twenty-six insulae. There were particularly active periods of building in Rome between 78 and 44BC and again from 31BC to 69AD.

The decline of the Roman appellation 'villa' was a long process, stretching into the shabby suburbia of a later century (see Chapter 4). In Rome at the height of its grandeur a villa was a fine country residence with spacious grounds; even if it was near a town, it had the character of a country retreat.

In the Antonine Itinerary, which lists 225 routes of the Roman Empire, mention is made of the *Rostrata Villa*, which was twenty-four miles outside Rome on the Via Flaminia. In Africa there were the *Villa Serviliana*, the *Villa Magna*, the *Villa Privata*, *Casas Villa Aniciorum*, the *Villa Fulgurita*, the *Vax Villa Repentina*, *Megradi Villa Aniciorum* and *Minna Villa Marsi*.

And it is with the Antonine Itinerary that we come to our first name for a house in England—the *Villa Faustini*, which stood near Scole at a staging point on the Roman road between Colchester and Caister St Edmunds. It was not a luxurious country seat but served rather as part of the network of imperial communications.

A good deal is known about some of the fine houses in the Roman Empire—and about some of their builders. Nero, like Augustus before him who had said he found the city of brick and left it of marble, set out to adorn Rome with magnificent buildings. One of these was the *Domus Transitoria* which linked the Imperial palace and the gardens of Maecenas. The great fire of AD64, which Nero himself was said to have started, destroyed the *Domus Transitoria* and the greater part of the city, and gave gave him the opportunity to build on an even grander scale. He replaced the *Domus Transitoria* with his *Golden House*, which was one of the wonders of Rome until it was destroyed by the Flavian emperors. The *Septizonum* of the Emperor Severus, with its seven stages of colonnades, was another notable palace.

Some of the other names by which houses of the Roman Empire have come to be known are traditional names which the original owners might not have recognised. The *House of Livia* on the Palatine in Rome is identified by some with the Empress Livia, because the inscription *Ivliv Avg(usta)* is stamped on lead pipes found in the excavations. Similarly *The House of the Vetti* at Pompeii is known to have belonged to A. Vettius Restitutus and A. Vettius Conviva.

Ostia, the seaport of Rome, was a favoured area, and many of the houses found there have been given characteristic names— *The House of Jupiter The Thunderer, The House of The Painted Vaults, The House of The Mosaic Niche, The House of The Gorgons.*

The Romans were great builders and administrators and there is still much evidence to be seen of their long period of rule. Their successors left nothing on a comparable scale; both the Saxons and the Normans built most of their ordinary homes from materials that have not lasted. The surviving names from this period therefore belong to a rather motley group of dwellings, several of which are still to be seen today: a pub, a priory, a couple of castles, and the unusually solid houses with which the Jewish community found it necessary to protect themselves and their possessions from fire, theft and attack.

Not far north of Basingstoke is *The Vyne*. No one knows how old this sunny and convivial name really is. It is mentioned in a deed of 1268, but almost everyone believes that the name is centuries older than this. It is thought to have added the role of an inn to that of a private house during at least some of its long history.

Chacombe Priory was the home of a Saxon lord called Bardi before William the Conqueror landed at Hastings.

In Lincoln there is the *Jew's House* dating from about 1150

AD, where the Jewess Balaset of Wallingford lived; she was hanged in 1290. *The Music House* at Norwich is believed to have been the home of Isaac the Jew, the great financier.

Croft Castle, a property mentioned in Domesday Book, is a Welsh Border castle which has been inhabited by the Croft family for 900 years. *Richmond Castle,* Britain's oldest stone castle, dates from about 1075, while Ireland's *Ferrycarrig Castle* dates from about 1180.

We owe one of the first grotesque names to the Normans, whose sense of humour apparently ran that way. One Bernard, who held various properties in the south of England, had a kindly friend who bestowed upon him the nickname of Paunch Face, and so he appears in Domesday Book as Bernard Pancevolt. One of the manors in Romsey became known as *Pauncefooteshill.*

Some of the names of London's early houses have come down to us—a London long before the Great Fire, whose narrow streets would be deserted at night except for a few stout characters venturing abroad with the help of smoky torches and the essential cudgel or sharp sword. Old City records recall lords and merchants, royal gifts and domestic accidents; and unforgettably in the 1570s:

> Kirkebeyes Castle and Fishers Follie.
> Spinilas Pleasure and Megses Glorie.

We shall come to Fisher and his Follie in due course.

Before that, with Stow's Survey of London as a guide, and a glance or two at the Calendar of Wills in the Court of Husting, we may learn of *Copped Hall* (or *La Coppedhalle*) in the parish of St John Walbrook, mentioned in 1285 and left, seven years later, by Roger de Dreyton to be sold for the poor; *The Erber,* so called since the middle of the 14th century, held by one Geoffrey Scroope by gift of Edward III; *Cokedon Hall* mentioned in 1316; and *Burley House* named after it was given to Sir Simon Burley.

Gerrardes Hall, whose gateways were built of Normandy stone, was originally called *Gisors Hall,* after the owner John Gisor,

Mayor of London, 1245, but the name was corrupted. A 40ft long pole in the hall was said to be the jousting staff of a giant who was alleged to have lived there.

The seeker whose family piety leads him to track down an ancestral home in old London must not be misled by the modern fetish of consistent spelling, especially during the period when the native English was asserting its claim to supersede French as the language of the court and of society. '*Cernettes Tower* or *Sernes Tower* in Bucklersburie, sometimes the king's house' was called *La Tower Servat* in 1331; *Sewtes Tour* 1358; *Surnetes Tour* 1365, elsewhere *Servers Tour*; *Sylvestre Tour* 1455 and in 1598 Stow calls it *Seruesse* or *Seruice Tower*. Then came a grocer named Buckle who knocked it down. His impiety had its reward: during the demolition he was hit by a piece of falling masonry and killed. His widow remarried and completed the rebuilding.

In the middle of the 14th century another successful grocer went by the resplendent name of Benedict de Folsham, and called his home *The Ringed Hall*. Almost 200 years later Henry VIII gave it to his goldsmith, and later it passed into the hands of Rewley Abbey, Oxford.

Blacke Hall in Wood Street (itself a very ancient name, thought to have been derived from the sale of wood there—a Michael 'de Wodestrate' is referred to in 1160) goes back at least as far as 1361 to a tenement called *Blackhalle*.

Many houses were named from the family to which they belonged—*Arundell House,* owned by the Earl of Arundel; *Essex House* where the Earl of Essex lodged; *Exeter House,* the London lodging of the Bishops of Exeter; *Leicester House,* built by Robert Dudley, Earl of Leicester.

Bay Hall on the corner of Bassinges Hall Streete belonged to a mercer named Thomas Bradbery. After his death in 1509 part of the house became a market house for the sale of 'woollen bays, watmols, flanels and such like'.

And so to *Fishers Follie* and *Megses Glorie*. John Kirkby, who

15

built *Kirkebeyes Castle* upon Bednall Greene, is said to have died of 'surrfaite' around 1578. What had begun as his castle later came to be known as *The Blind Beggar's House.* Jasper Fisher, who built *Fishers Follie* at about the same time, seems to have been no more inclined than Kirkby to deny himself the good things of life. Described as a man 'of no greater calling, possession or wealth' and in debt to many, he built a large and beautiful house complete with pleasure gardens and bowling alleys.

Benedict Spinola was a successful Italian merchant who enclosed some land about 1574. The land is thought to have been developed into gardens which became known as *Spinilas Pleasure.*

Megses Glorie was probably a house near *Kirkebeyes Castle.* If the unknown rhymester was consistent in his aim, then the owner of *Megses Glorie* too may have been an exponent of the art of living now and paying later.

Henry VIII kept what is referred to as a 'mint of coynage' at *Southwarke Place*, a house built by Charles Brandon, Duke of Suffolk, and formerly known as *Suffolk House.* This was later given to the Archbishop of York to compensate for *York House* near Westminster which Henry had taken from Cardinal Wolsey. Eventually the Archbishop sold it to merchants and it was pulled down and cottages built in its place.

One of the most important houses in Easte Cheape, *The Garland*, became a brewhouse and was finally divided into small tenements. A number of great houses were divided into tenements. *Barklies Inne*, built by the Lord of Barkley and lodging of the Earl of Warwick in Henry VI's reign, was eventually let out in several tenements; *The Leaden Porch* was divided into a tavern and a merchants' house; and another house, *The Old Wardrobe*, was divided into small houses for Jews, and later pulled down.

The word 'wardrobe' seems to have been quite a popular name at one time, and the explanation that it was not merely a cupboard but a hanging room adjoining a bedroom hardly accounts

16

for this. *Northumberland House*, Aldersgate, given to Queen Jane by Henry IV, became known as *Queen Jane's Wardrobe*, before it finally became a printing house. Yet another was known as *The Queen's Wardrobe*. This had once been *Tower Royall*, lodging place of King Stephen, and the house to which the mother of Richard II fled when rebels took possession of the Tower of London.

The King's Great Wardrobe, built in the mid-14th century in the parish of St Andrews by Sir John Beauchampe, was sold to Edward III. The parson of St Andrews complained that he had lost a lot of tithes from property demolished to make room for the great house, and the King granted him forty shillings a year in perpetuity as compensation. It is thought that secret letters and confidential business concerning the Crown estates were dealt with here.

First called *Le Barge* in a deed of 1414, *The Old Barge* was a stone and timber house that got its name because barges were rowed up the Walbroke behind the house from the Thames.

The Hanse merchants owned *Easterlings Hall* and it was known by this name until the early 15th century, when they bought nearby tenements and the Stileyerd or Stilehof, and for the next hundred years the area was known as *Styleyerd*.

Mountjoye Place had more than one name. Originally belonging to the Church, it was let to the Mountjoys and then to a Cambridge College for lodgings. It was occupied by the Association or College of Doctors of Civil Law in London, when it became known as *Doctors Commons*. Both *Gristes House* (home of one Griste) and *The Green Gate*, a 'fayre old house' in Limestreet Warde and home of Alderman Malpas, were the scenes of robberies carried out in the mid-15th century by Jacke Cade, captain of the Rebels in Kent. *The Weyhouse*, Cornhill Ward, was where merchandise for overseas was weighed at the King's Beam. *Cold Harbrough*, once the property of the Black Prince, was let to a draper in the reign of Edward II at thirty-three

17

B

shillings a year. *The Manor of the Rose* was purchased to found the Merchant Taylors School in 1561.

In the 17th century the boundaries of certain London Wards were sometimes referred to by the names of the houses in the streets—'. . . from a cook's house called *The Sign of King David* . . . into *Huntington House*. . . from a cook's house called *The Blew Boor* . . .'

All these names and many more once graced the streets of London, and happily some splendid names still survive today, though often slightly changed: *Stourton House,* Totehill Street, home of the last Lord of Dacre of the South, survives today in Strutton Ground.

It might be expected that Oxford, with its genius for survivals and revivals, should have preserved some memorable names. In former times any house of average size could be called a hall; for a building to be known as someone's Hall did not imply that it was a vast mansion or an academic hall. It might have been an inn or an ordinary home. *Coventry Hall* later became *The Roebuck*. No one knowing Oxford will be surprised to find that it included both *Hell*—'a messuage &c called *Hell*; rent 6s 8d per annum'—and *The Seven Deadly Sinnes. Hell* was either a gambling hell or a cluster of small tenements in a place called Hell Passage, about the end of the 18th century. Oxford also had a *Moses Hall, Perilous Hall* (1324), *Rack Hall* and *Saucer Hall.* In 1320 the tenement of John de Dokelinton was known as *Dokelinton's Inn*; the Post Office stands on the site today.

A property called *Bachelor's Tower* was mentioned in 1581. Nobody seems to know the origin of the name. It was part of the defences of the town and belonged to the City. In 1715 it was occupied by the man in charge of the waterworks which had been built in 1695; meanwhile it had acquired the name of *Friar Bacon's Study.*

Oxford provides us with at least one fine example of the way in which names can change through the years. About 1360 the city is thought to have acquired a property in Berkshire, in the parish of South Hinksey, to be a place of residence for the man who repaired the causeway from Folly Bridge to Bagley Wood. Because the property was opposite the Chapel of St Nicholas it was first called *St Nicholas Yard*, but as the man who mended the road was always a hermit, it came to be called *The Hermitage*; it was also called *Bridwright's Place*. In 1565 a lease of '*the Armytage*' was granted to Thomas Ryley for twenty-one years at a rent of 10s. And so through the years the property changed hands, but has survived in a recognisable form; the eleven houses of which it consists today were built about 1860. As late as 1926 they were still known as *Grandpont Villas*. Though the houses are now simply known as Nos 65-85 Abingdon Road, the name *Grandpont* is still to be found on a house nearby.

Frewen Hall, formerly the *Bridewell* of Oxford, was the home during the 18th century of Dr Frewen who was famous both for his excellence as a physician and for the number of his wives.

In other parts of England there were memorable names; *Marlepins* in Shoreham, the toll house where the Lords of Shoreham received their taxes and harbour dues; *Yaverland* in the Isle of Wight; *Fish House* and *Paycockes*.

A fine house, whose ambitious (and presumably devout) owner built it as a copy of the great church of San Vitale in Ravenna, was named *La Ronde*, which for us recalls not the piety of the Emperor Justinian but the amorous intrigues of a popular film.

Another attempt to find propitious association for the name of a house was that of Sir Thomas Tresham, who started building *Lyveden New Bield* ('bield' meaning a place of shelter) to symbolise the Passion. It was not, alas, to prove a shelter to him; he became involved in the Gunpowder Plot and did not finish the house. The conspirators were seized at *Holbeach House*, Kingswinford, where Percy and Catesby were killed.

Other English houses have had happier associations and distinctions. *Brympton D'Evercy* has the longest straight staircase in England, and *Layer Marney Tower* the highest Tudor gate-

19

house. *Packwood House* has a yew tree garden of about 1650 which was planted to commemorate the Sermon on the Mount; and *Temple of the Winds* is so called because the house is modelled on the Temple of the Winds in Athens.

Tastes change, and fashions in names reflect this. The names in this chapter would have become attached to a house by popular repute, recorded more or less accurately in deeds and correspondence at fairly wide intervals of time, but most of the people who used the names must have carried them in their heads—the ordinary passer-by could not have read the name, and the penny post was many years in the future.

Today you might be unlikely to call your house *Copped Hall*, *Friar Bacon's Study*, *The Seven Deadly Sins*, or *Queen Jane's Wardrobe*, but *The Old Barge* or *The Green Gate* would certainly not look out of place. Human nature is still fairly weak, and I admit that if I had a fine enough house, the irresistible swagger of *Megses Glorie* might flaunt itself once more.

CHAPTER 3

Famous People and Famous Houses

From Nero's *Golden House* to Ian Fleming's *Goldeneye*—although Commander James Bond preferred the anonymity of numbers, his creator chose to name his own house.

What names do the famous and successful choose for their houses? Wealth may make it more desirable as well as more difficult to avoid publicity, but fortunately for this inquiry, the famous (and the infamous) are not all hidden behind unnamed doors.

Paul Getty bought *Sutton Place* in England, *Castello Di Paulo* in Italy, but in the United States lives at 17985 Pacific Coast Highway.

Not all wealthy Americans stick entirely to numbers. Many have country properties as well. For instance, Henry Ford II has *Gross Point Farms*, the Mellons have *Huntland Downs* and among the Rockefellers' addresses is *Poncantico Hills*. But for sheer panache *The Great House*, Roaring River takes some beating.

Buckingham Palace has over the years had four other official names and at least one unofficial one. *Goring House* was the original house built on the site in the 17th century by Lord

21

Goring; burnt down in 1674 it was replaced by *Arlington House*, named after its builder Lord Arlington; it was acquired by the Marquis of Normanby, soon to be Duke of Buckingham, and so became *Buckingham House*. When George II bought it in 1761 he preferred to call it *The Queen's House*. Not content with all this, the general public affectionately dubbed it *Pimlico Palace*. It might even have become the Houses of Parliament had William IV's offer been accepted when the then Houses of Parliament were burned down in 1834.

Several legends lie behind the name of *Holyrood Palace* in Scotland, most of them concerning the casket known as the Black Rood of Scotland, said to hold a piece of the Cross of Christ. An abbey was founded in Edinburgh in 1128, and the casket kept there fore safety; the abbey became known as *Holyrood*. The palace of today, whose chapel is the resting place of several of the kings of Scotland, was begun in 1501 and rebuilt after the fire of 1650. It is a name whose beauty and tranquillity have long outlived the murder of Rizzio by jealous followers of Lord Darnley, who disliked his friendship with Mary Queen of Scots.

Other Royal residences include *Windsor Castle* (the largest inhabited castle in the world), *Balmoral Castle*, *Sandringham House Clarence House*, *The Castle of Mey*, *Royal Lodge*, *Kensington Palace*, *York House*, the Duke of Kent's *Coppins*, *Barnwell Manor*, one of the homes of the Duke of Gloucester, and Princess Alexandra's *Thatched House Lodge*.

Anne Boleyn and Katherine Howard are alleged to have taken lovers from *Old Soar*, home of their relatives the Culpepers, and almost the only surviving manor house from the period around 1300. Anne also stayed at *Hever Castle*. Lady Jane Grey once lived at the fifteenth-century *Seymour Court*, and *Hatfield House* for a time was the home of Queen Elizabeth I.

Hellen's, the old manorial house lived in since 1292, received visits from the Black Prince and Bloody Mary, and *Berkeley Castle*, built in 1153 and the oldest inhabited castle in England, had the doubtful privilege of witnessing the murder of Edward II.

While some houses have achieved lasting fame on account of the great men who occupied them—Sir Winston Churchill's *Chartwell*, and *Hughenden Manor*, home of Disraeli—others are known today for different reasons—*Beaulieu Abbey* and *Palace House*, owned by Lord Montagu are now renowned for their vintage car museum; *Woburn Abbey*'s Wild Animal Kingdom is ideal for a family outing; *Badminton*, which gave its name to the game, is now associated with equestrian events, and *Chequers* is the country home of the British Prime Minister.

Away from the surroundings most usually associated with them, famous men sometimes prefer a quietly memorable simplicity. After the achievements of the Everest expedition Lord Hunt's choice of *Highway Cottage* has a certain piquancy. And *La Boisserie* was somehow part of the dignity and simplicity which distinguished the private life of General de Gaulle.

The birthplaces and homes of the famous have not always had names remarkable enough to attract the attention of historians or biographers. This is a pity, because even an ordinary name brings a scene closer to us: we can think of Sir Walter Raleigh planting the first potato at *Myrtle Grove*, and 'Carcase' Morley, the butcher whose land speculations made him a national figure and a target for Prior, Gay and Pope, sporting a family crest showing a butcher holding a pole-axe, but contenting himself with the relatively sober name of *Blue Bridge House* for his home at Halstead.

Who will follow in their footsteps, and why will they be remembered? Will it be George and Ringo, who have *Friar Park* and *Round Hill*? Will it be Mrs Henry M. Flager of *Whitehall*, the world's best-dressed woman of the pre-1914 era who had her wardrobes moth-proofed although she was said never to wear a dress a second time?

Some contemporary figures have houses with unusual names—Fernandel chose the exotic *Ville Les Milleroses*; Prince Sadruddin Aga Khan *Chateau de Bellerive* (*Bellerive* also being the name of Claudette Colbert's home); Celia Johnson has the delightful *Merriemoles House*. But many choose very simple names

—Baroness Wootton lives at *High Barn*, Benjamin Britten at *The Red House*, Malcolm Muggeridge at *Park Cottage*, Jack Hawkins at *Westmead Lodge*, Jacques Cousteau at *Villa Richard*.

The name chosen by Frank Lloyd Wright for the house he built in Wisconsin was singularly appropriate. *Taliesin North* was built on the brow of a hill and was named after a Welsh bard called Taliesin, which means 'shining brow'.

One of the world's most famous people living in one of the world's most famous houses is, of course, the President of the United States of America in *The White House*. This is the oldest federal building in Washington and although it was not until Theodore Roosevelt's time that it became known officially as *The White House*, yet even before it was painted white after being burnt by the British in 1814 it was gradually, if unofficially, acquiring that name from the colour of the limestone used in its construction. Sometimes it was also referred to as *The Executive Mansion*.

It is the hope of many successful men that they will come to be known simply by their initials. You still have to be very well known, though, to call one of your homes the *LBJ Ranch*.

But it is the writers who collect the most memorable names. Shakespeare's *Anne Hathaway's Cottage*, *Hall's Croft*, *Mary Arden's House* and *New Place* are well enough known, and he is supposed to have poached at *Charlecote Park*, but how well known is *Gawsworth Hall*? This was the home of Mary Fitton, Maid of Honour at the Court of Queen Elizabeth I, who may have been the 'dark lady' of the sonnets.

With the exception of *Sandy Knowe Farm* ('knowe'—a mound) the early childhood home of Scott, we seem to know very little of the way in which such houses as Mrs Browning's *Hope End* got their names. *Bleak House*, the favourite home of Charles Dickens where he is said to have written 'David Copperfield', has, in spite of its chilly, uninviting sound, had many imitators. One of Alfred Lord Tennyson's homes was *Farringford*, now a hotel, on the Isle of Wight, and *Aldworth* was another. Henry

James lived at *Lamb House*, and the Wordsworths had several houses—among them *Rydal Mount* and *Dove Cottage*. Coleridge lived at *Alfoxden*; the Brontes' *Haworth Parsonage* took its name from the moorland village where it was situated; *Moor Park* was associated with Swift; Charles Darwin lived at *Down House* and Sir Isaac Newton was born at *Woolsthorpe Manor*.

Rudyard Kipling described the surroundings of his house—*Bateman's*—in 'Puck of Pook's Hill' and 'Rewards and Fairies'. After World War I Lawrence of Arabia made his home at *Clouds Hill*, and Beatrix Potter bought a 17th-century house called *Hill Top*.

There is no hint of mysterious footprints or treacherous butlers about a name like *Winterbrook House*, the home of Agatha Christie, and *Heath House* provides a comfortingly terrestrial base for the science fiction of Brian Aldiss. Apart from Kingsley Amis's *Lemmons*, many present day authors choose straightforward names like *The Mead* (John Betjeman), *The Holt* (John Braine) and *Ashcombe House* (Asa Briggs).

Two famous Americans with ancestral homes in Britain are George Washington—his forefathers had *Sulgrave Manor*—and John Harvard, founder of the university, whose mother lived in *Harvard House*. Thomas Jefferson turned to Italy for inspiration, and when he completed the home he had planned for years, called it *Monticello*, Italian for 'little mountain'.

Some houses are famous in themselves because of the events associated with them. One of the people closely connected with building the original *Burton Agnes Hall*, in Yorkshire, was Ann Griffiths, and it was her gruesome wish that her skull should remain in the house after her death. Over the years a legend grew up that if anyone tried to remove it the house would be filled with blood-curdling screams. Finally the occupants ensured that the skull remained in the house by bricking it into one of the walls.

Uppark distinguishes a 17th-century house on a hill from its neighbouring 'Downpark'. The young H. G. Wells is said to

25

have produced some of his earliest work there.

The oak tree that hid Charles II in the grounds of *Boscobel House* must be the most famous tree in history, if the number of modern houses called *Boscobel* is anything to judge by. But this was not his only refuge—he hid in the chapel of *Ancient House*, and was also sheltered at *Moseley Old Hall*. It seems only natural that the house where he stayed on his restoration to the throne in May 1660 should be known as *Restoration House*.

Some names come from the family or from the district in which they were built, and the original name of the land can often be found in the Domesday Book. But others have entirely different origins, some obscure. *Blenheim Palace*, home of the Marlboroughs and birthplace of Sir Winston Churchill, was built on land given to the first Duke of Marlborough, John Churchill, by Queen Anne as a reward for defeating Louis XIV's troops near a village on the Danube called Blindheim (or Blenheim). *Longleat* took its name from the long 'leat' or watercourse which fed the nearby lake, and *Compton Wynyates* is thought to have derived its name from the 'wind gate'.

Owlpen Manor; *Bedgebury Pinetum*; *Lytes Carfy*; *Purse Caundle Manor*; *Sadborow*; *Quar Wood*; *Maison Dieu House*; *Hyde Crook*; *Charpitor*—marvellous names that have been preserved for hundreds of years, and ones which must surely belong to one house alone. It would be something of an anticlimax to find *Temple Newsam* or *Castle Howard* adorning the gate of a chalet bungalow of 1970 vintage.

Every country in the world has historic buildings with interesting names—although 'old' in Australia, for example, can mean 150 years, whereas 'old' in Egypt might refer to buildings like the funerary temples known as the *Castles of Millions of Years* dating back to the time of the Pharaohs.

Although most of the world-famous buildings referred to here are homes on a very grand scale, yet some of their names have been borrowed by home owners around the world—names like *Sans Souci* (carefree), the summer residence of Frederick the

Great in East Germany, or *The House in the Wood* (*Huis Ten Bosch*) in The Hague, used by Queen Juliana.

Houses become famous for a variety of reasons. Perhaps they are now used as art galleries or museums—like the beautiful *Mauritshuis* in The Hague. Named after its first inhabitant, Count Johan Maurits, later Prince of Nassau, it now houses a superb collection of pictures. The name of *Gunterstein*, in Breuken, Holland, has survived for nearly six hundred years, although the present house was rebuilt in the 17th century. *Potok* in Poland was even earlier. Once the seat of the Potocki family, its history goes back to the 13th century. Five centuries later one of the Potockis employed 10,000 labourers to build a castle for his wife Sophia—*The Castle of Sofiyorsky*.

The King of Poland used to live in *Wawel Castle*, built on the hill of Wawel overlooking Cracow. The Palace of the Empress Catherine the Great of Russia was first given a name meaning 'elevated spot', but this was later changed to *Tsarskoe Selo*—'the village of the Tsars'. *Sarospatak*, the centuries-old fortified home built for the kings of Hungary near the town of that name, has a most remarkable 'fighting floor' sandwiched between the upper and lower floors, to enable a watch to be kept through apertures in its thick walls.

Very familiar, since it appears on the label of the Mateus Rosé bottle, is the *Solar Mateus* ('Solar'—manor house), one of the largest mansions in Portugal. Although it is disappointing to find that the grapes from the nearby vineyards are not actually turned into wine at the back of the house but in a modern factory not far away, yet its cool, low rooms full of interesting family history are a delight to visit on a scorchingly hot day.

When you visit the *Casa de Pilatos* among the narrow alleys in the centre of Seville you may be told that it is named after Pilate's house in Jerusalem. Begun about 1480 for Pedro Enriques de Rivera, it was continued by the first Marquis of Tarifa who, according to the legend, visited the Holy Land and was so deeply impressed by Pilate's house that he built his on the same plan.

Standing in a vast park high above Rome to catch all the fresh winds from the sea, *Belrispiro* was aptly named. It was built in the seventeenth century for Camillo Pamphilj, nephew of Pope Innocent X, but it was subsequently bought by the State from the Doria family and is now an ambassador's residence. Its original name has been changed to the old family names and it is now known as the *Villa Doria-Pamphilj*.

Bulgarian houses are mostly numbered, but a few houses of particular significance or historic importance bear names. Enclosed by a high wall in the old Bulgarian city of Plovdiv stands one of the most beautiful houses I have ever visited—*Kojumdzioglu House*, so called because it once belonged to Argir Kojumdzioglu. It was built by Hajji Georgi of Constantinople in 1847 and its graceful frontage follows the shape of a yoke for carrying buckets. Once used as a tobacco warehouse, it has now been restored to its former glory and its long low rooms house a first-class ethnographic exhibition. Georgi also built another very fine house in Plovdiv—*Georgiadi House*, now the Museum of the National Liberation; and not far away is *Dancov House*, once the home of Georgi Dancov, a well known painter of the Bulgarian Renaissance.

You might be rather puzzled to find an Italianate villa named *Buchlovice* in the centre of Czechoslovakia, but in the seventeenth century John Peterswaldsky's wife-to-be refused to live in his ancestral home, *Buchlov Castle,* and would only marry him on condition that he build her a new house in the Italian style.

King Ludwig II of Bavaria was obsessed with building, and planned enormous romantic castles in various parts of his kingdom, to the detriment of the country's finances. Unfortunately at the time of his death only *Linderhof* had been completed. *Schloss Herrenchiemsee*, the castle that was to be like Versailles, on an island in the middle of Lake Herrenchiemsee near Traunstein, has only two bedrooms. Before he could finish it he was certified insane. As he hated people, and wouldn't even have servants near him (the dining table disappeared through the floor to be cleared and re-set), very few saw the castle during his lifetime, but it is now a great attraction to visitors.

Some great European houses have been taken over by international organisations. Among them are *Berlaymont,* the seat of the European Commission in Brussels; *Kirchberg,* the skyscraper in Luxembourg housing the secretariat of the European Parliament; *Chateau de la Muette* in Paris, home of the Organisation for Economic Co-operation and Development; *Maison de l'Europe,* home of the Council of Europe in Strasbourg, and *Ravenstein* in Brussels, which houses the secretariat of the Council of Ministers.

It might be appropriate to end this chapter with *Kronberg,* the castle at Elsinore which is usually thought of as the original setting of the Hamlet legend. It was once called *Krogon,* but in 1577 it was decreed that the name should be changed and anyone misusing the new name was required to pay a fine of a good ox! A proper regard for a name—a fine of a good ox might well be levied today for some of the house-names described in later chapters.

CHAPTER 4

Changing Tastes:
With a Look at Two English Towns

We have seen how those early house names that still survive can bring back the atmosphere and the fashions of a vanished era.

As we draw nearer to our own time we can ask ourselves whether the development of modern cities and suburbs, the growth of home ownership, the tremendous new markets in house property opened up by building societies and estate agents, and other social and economic changes, brought any changes of fashion in the choice of names.

Today there are, simply, thousands more houses and hence thousands more names. One's little individual flag of identity waves among a thousand others. Two reactions may be expected. One is that of a new type of snob who regards any sort of name as vulgar and simply relies on the unanswerable fact of 'a good address': the right number in the right street or square must be left to speak for itself—and preferably not reveal, as it did to Lady Bracknell in 'The Importance of Being Earnest', that the address is on 'the unfashionable side'.

Where such self-evident prestige cannot be hoped for, one

might expect a tendency towards the outlandish or outrageous type of name; this type of name which attempts to relieve many rather characterless houses seems to be a comparatively modern manifestation.

In the first part of this chapter changing tastes are examined by comparing three main groups of houses built at different dates. The earliest group were built around the turn of the century, the second group were built between the two world wars when estates built by 'spec' builders began to appear on the perimeter of towns throughout the country, and the third group comes from the huge developments that have taken place since the last war—housing estates (many of which are of the open-plan design with no gates on which to hang a name) and the vast amount of in-filling that has taken place, often in the gardens of large, old houses.

Although many of the modern estate houses have little to distinguish one from another, except perhaps the shape of the front window or the colour of the up-and-over garage door, only a small proportion of them have names. On the other hand, many of the larger detached homes built on spare pieces of land or in former orchards have names. Several reasons for this suggest themselves. The numbering of an old road will have been done many years ago and the new house on half of somebody else's garden will therefore have to carry an A or a B after the number of the original house. This immediately suggests that the house is merely an appendage, or else that you live in the upstairs flat. A name on such a house becomes essential. Alternatively, the smaller new house on a large estate may, for some people, be merely a first step in home ownership and tend to be regarded as more of a transit site, and naming may be postponed until the owners have moved into something with a little more individuality. It may, too, be a sheer necessity to use a number to enable the postman to find one postbox among so many similar ones.

Old large houses in their own grounds built around the turn of the century frequently carry names—*The Rookery, The*

Hollies, St Audrey's; but at that time thousands of houses were built in terraces, many just for renting, and here the pattern is usually different. Either they just bear numbers or else the entire terrace has its own name as well as a street name—Abbey Terrace, Springfield Street, may have twenty or more houses as separate entities.

Where an old house has a name, this was sometimes actually carved in the stonework on the entrance porch—*Stokesley*; *Glenville*; *Seighford Cottage*; or else painted on the fanlight above the front door—*Hill View*; *Eversleigh*; *Wentworth*. In many cases, although the name still remains it is not actually used in the address, the owners preferring just the number and street name.

Where houses were built in pairs rather than in long terraces, they frequently share a stone plaque let into the brickwork near the eaves bearing legends like *Fern Villas* or *West View*, with the date when the houses were built, and sometimes the initials of the builder. Here the houses must use numbers as well to avoid confusion.

The small house of this type, often in a rather stuffy area of suburbia, would frequently be described as a 'villa'. The use of 'villa' carried to the very last an implied claim to superiority, though the superior qualities once found in a 'villa' had become ever more remote. By the turn of the century, the word 'villadom' had come to be used for a certain type of smug and genteel suburban life. The decline and fall of the Roman spaciousness and amenity were complete.

By far the richest harvest of names in a street of houses of varying ages will be found in those built in the 1930s. Perhaps this reflects the growth between the wars of the speculative builder and the semi-detached suburbia he largely created in which, however, home ownership was still a matter for considerable pride and satisfaction.

Many of the between-the-wars estate houses looked alike, although individual front gardens distinguished one from another perhaps to a greater extent than the usual expanse of turf found on many open-plan developments today. But for thousands of people here for the first time was a status symbol, and it could well be that the choice of name added to the glamour. What type of name did people choose? The variety is notably wide. Villa, Lodge, Place and View are less favoured than in earlier years, and foreign place names were not so often chosen as they are today. Holiday memories have always been popular, but as the great boom in packaged holidays to the Continent did not take place until after World War II it is names like *Lynton* (with sometimes *Lynmouth* next door), *Rottingdean*, *Lyme Regis*, *Clevedon* or *Torquay* that recur again and again. Local beauty spots and other rural associations referred to in Chapters 9 and 11 apply, and many a 1930s house sports *Windrush*, *The Chase*, *Exmoor* or *Spring Bank*. There were a few jokes—*Updown*, *The Knock*, *Justakot*, *Mywaye*, *Dunlukin*, *Trail End*—but perhaps not as many attempts at humour as there are today. Very few chose the British seaside towns that attracted millions—places like Blackpool, Morecambe, Llandudno or Brighton.

Not all new houses have modern names, of course. People still choose names of the well-tried *Greengates*, *Greytiles*, *Meadowcroft* and *Tree View* variety, but it is very noticeable that foreign place names or phrases from foreign languages have crept in—which, after all, is only to be expected with the increase in foreign travel. There have always been French names—think of the number of *Chez Nous* and *Mon Repos* there are, even in Portugal and India, and to these have been added other French names such as *Maison d'Amour*, *Petits Fleurs*, *Le Roi*, *Le Nid*, *La Maison*, *Maison Bleu*, *Petit Amour*, *Très Joli*, *Le Chalet* or *Gai Séjour*. However, there does seem to be a growing preference (and particularly on the very modern expensive developments) for *Casa*, either on its own or followed by another word—*Casa Mia*, *Casa Alegre*, *Casa Mereno*; even *Casa Nova*.

Latin and the Romance languages have suggested *Dulce Domum*, *Bon Vista*, *Cede Deo*, *Domus*, *Los Arcos*, *Nostra Casa*, *Piazza Amerina*, *Quando*, *Que Sera*, *S'Agaro* and *Sol-y-Vista*. But

33

c

although many names have come from the Continent, and many foreign words for 'house' have supplanted 'villa'—*Chalet de la Fontaine, Casa Pedro, Maison Blanche*—yet the Portuguese custom of preceding a name by 'Vivenda' (*Vivenda Luzdivina*) has not, as yet, caught on.

Marriage and home ownership come at an earlier age nowadays, and this may be reflected in a greater willingness to splash out with ingenious names such as *Coromandel* (where the Yonghi Bonghi Bo lived), *Kota Tingii* (from Malaysia), *Yuyu* (from China), or *Abyan* (from Aden).

While it is easy to generalise about changing patterns in house names and quote a few at random, a closer look at a single community should reveal whether there is anything in the idea that, just as fashions change in consumer goods, so they do in house names.

Therefore a rather closer study has been made of two towns. A number of factors have to be taken into account before areas can be chosen for study. Ideally, the town should have developed slowly over the past six or seven hundred years and have been inhabited by a number of wealthy families. This will mean that records of properties are available, frequently with names. A wider variety of development is likely to have taken place, particularly in properties listed in early records as 'Private Residences of the Gentry' than in an area that underwent rapid expansion at the time of the Industrial Revolution, when thousands of unnamed back-to-back houses all jammed together in little streets, or one-up-and-one-down houses built around a courtyard, suddenly sprang up.

The two towns selected are Abingdon, with its flourishing wool trade in the Middle Ages, dominated by the Abbey until the Dissolution, and Cheltenham, once a wealthy spa town, home of retired Colonial Service personnel, and now much influenced by modern industrial development.

Abingdon is a small town in Berkshire of some 18,000 people, with a fascinating history. Today its main industries are car

34

assembly, brewing, printing, the manufacture of leather goods, and there is a large scientific research establishment in the neighbourhood. Until the seventeenth century it had a rich trade in wool and cloth, and until the Dissolution (the Abbey was surrendered to the king in February 1538) the town was dominated by the Abbey. A great deal of work is being done to preserve its treasures and to record its history, and thus we have a record of some of its very early houses and the origins of their names.

Recently a large housing development known as the Fitzharris Estate was built on land received by the Norman Knight Owen at the time of the Conquest. His great-great-grandson Hugh, son of Henry and so known as Hugh FitzHarry, eventually sold the land and the dwelling known as *Fitzharris* (or *Fitzharry's*) *Farm* back to the Abbey, and although the last Fitzharris manor house was demolished in 1954 the name Fitzharris still continues. There was also at one time a *Fitzharris Cottage* which might have been an old toll house.

At the end of the fifteenth century part of the Fitzharris estate was separated to form *Lacies Court,* thought to have been named after an early lessee, and some two hundred years later even more land was carved out for *Heythornes* or *Hawthornes* which then became *Oliver's Farm,* and then *The Gables.* From the Abbey manor of Northcourt a farm was let off which was known by the names of its succeeding tenants—*Keepe's Farm, Lynges Farm* and then *Goodlucks.*

Barton Court was originally *Le Berton,* and outside the Abbey precinct until 1372 when the servants became parishioners of St Nicholas and the farm became part of the Abbey. It was destroyed in the Civil War, but it has subsequently been replaced, altered and restored yet again. In 1554 there was a tenement called *Le Lyon* in what was later Turnagain Lane, but this may well have been an inn. In 1578 William Blacknall, a miller, made his home at *The Garner* which he had purchased as part of the Abbey site from the Crown after the Dissolution. The Blacknall family also bought *Master Stone's Lodgings,* another sixteenth-century name derived from Master Stone, thought to have been the last Abbot's brother-in-law who was living at the Abbey at the time of the Dissolution. The name stuck long after his death and the house was eventually rebuilt and became the home of William Blacknall, son of the miller.

In Henry V's reign *Banbery Court* was the mansion of the bridge builder John Banberie, and it was here that the feasts of the Fraternity of the Cross were held until the Vicar of Bray gave them a separate Feast House.

The Malt House takes its name from the fact that in the seventeenth century the site became a wharfage for malt and in due course was occupied by the Tomkins family as the headquarters of their flourishing malt trade. They also built *Twickenham House, Clock House* and *Stratton House* (now offices).

Waste Court probably began as a nickname as it took its name from a dwelling house built in the eighteenth century on a piece of waste 'where before was a dunghill'. Old leases refer to properties called *The Tallow House* and *Chickens.*

Caldecott House was named from the manorial lands and homestead known as Caldecott which were part of the manor of St Helen's founded just after the Norman Conquest. The word itself is of considerable antiquity and is generally associated with cold, cheerless hovels or dwellings in exposed places, but sometimes refers also to a place where travellers could shelter from the cold.

One very old name which has been revived is that of *The Cosener's House,* and although today it relates to a red-bricked hostel, the house is on the site of what was once the Abbey Kitchener's; hence Cuisinier's and so Cosener's.

Before passing on to more modern times, mention must be made of *Burford House,* the name of the public lavatory maintained by the Corporation from the time when the town was freed from the power of the Abbey. Although the population was only then between one and two thousand, in 1584 the Borough arranged for a lease to be

'. . . graunted to Willyam Kysbe gent. of a peace of waste
growmd whereuppon Burford house which is a common
priveye is by hym newe Builded. . . .'

One wonders how many more such public amenities (with or
without grand names) were erected by enlightened councils.

One of the main streets in Abingdon is Ock Street, so called
from the river which flows parallel to it. It has been known by
this name in one form or another (Okkestrete, Okstret) since the
middle of the thirteenth century, although it was derived from a
pre-Saxon word 'ehoc' meaning salmon. A hundred years ago
the street was a mixture of private residences and trading establishments, such as the rope maker, the maltster, the fancy repository and the grocer and tea dealer (who also acted as registrar of
births and deaths). Early records show no house numbers, merely
residents' names and house names where appropriate. Thus in
1890 there were *Clock House, Havenhope, Oriel House, The
Acacias* and *Piccadilly House*. Four years later *The Acacias* was
changed to *Helenstowe* (after a nearby nunnery established before
700AD) and has remained so ever since. *Havenhope* became
Ockholme in 1905, but subsequently the house disappeared
altogether. In 1906 *Cranley House* came and a year later No 50
acquired the name of *Berwyn*. By 1930 several of these old names
had gone, but there were one or two new ones—*Perth House* and
Ock House.

By 1970 great changes had taken place. Many of the houses
had been demolished to make way for supermarkets, garages,
coal yards or blocks of flats, and many of them had had their
fronts removed and replaced by shop windows. For example, the
former *Ocklea* had become part of a brewery; the splendid town
house called *Clock House* remained but part of it had been
divided into *Clock Cottage* and *Clock House Flat*. A taxi service
operated from *The Beaconsfield* (whose name was carved in stone
over the door and decorated with three stone versions of Disraeli's
head). *Oriel House* had become Oriel Hotel. A furniture store had
Walton House painted on its fanlight; there was an *Appledore*

37

Cottage next to a smart antique shop, and an old house at the end of the road was called *The Dobbins,* but the other names had disappeared.

With the growth of industry the town developed and some fairly expensive property was put up within easy reach of the town centre, particularly in the 1920-30s. One of the main roads out of Abingdon is an excellent example of changing fashions. In 1890 there were eighteen private residences, among them *Rose Cottage, Bleak House, The Firs, St Joseph's Villa, Barton Lodge* and *Bradbury Villa.* In 1893 *Bleak House* became *Rámkátorá,* and three years later *Jessamine Villa* became *The Retreat* and shortly afterwards *Landour.* A few years later No 3 became *Ivy Cottage* and then on to the scene came *Dovedale, Casnewydd, The Bungalow* and *Fern Villa.*

Between 1922 and 1930 real changes took place. *Ivy Cottage* and *The Firs* disappeared and a whole rash of new names appeared: *Ribston Villa, Boundary House, New House, High Tree House,* and many names which illustrate the trend towards giving a house a single name without the previously fashionable appendages such as Villa, Lodge, House—*Tullyhunco, Wandilla, Tenby, Virginia, Whitley, Cholsey, Alstowe, Thornwood, Trevethin, Lechlade* and *Hawthorne.*

A few of these names still survive but many have been added in the ensuing years—the older houses bearing names such as *Rose Bank, Wayside, Wychwood, Elmstead* and *Red Roofs.* Many of the new houses as yet only have numbers, but while one or two have the more traditional names such as *The Orchard, Glendale, Charlbury,* the new and unusual are appearing—*Bohole, Corbeyrier, Coromandel.*

Round the corner past terrace houses built in the early 1900s and called *Hill View, Holly Lodge, Eversleigh* and *Mayfield* the town spreads out with *Lymington, Nutley, Bybrooke, Greenhedges, Riversdale, The Haven, Lyme Regis, Pinehurst, Speyside, Cheriton, Normandy* and *Cornerways,* until the piles of bricks and scaffolding and the newly laid roads are reached and here *Cartref* and *Aysgarth* have to make way for slices of timber on chains, wrought iron writing or other modern devices announcing *Naivasha*, *Olita*, *Hoe Hok*, *Tara*, *Kerrera* and *Casa Mereno*.

In many respects Cheltenham is entirely different from Abingdon—almost the whole of its development has taken place during the last three centuries and during that time its character has undergone more than one change. It is therefore perhaps all the more interesting to see whether the pattern of its house names differs from Abingdon.

Before the Conquest the area belonged to Edward the Confessor, and until the Dissolution it seems to have passed through the hands of people like the Earl of Hereford who exchanged it for other lands, the Earl of Salisbury who leased the benefit of the markets and fairs to the inhabitants, his son who forfeited his estates to the Crown, the wife of Henry III, the Abbey of Pischam in Normandy, until at the time of the Dissolution it was owned by a nunnery in Middlesex.

Until the beginning of the eighteenth century it was a very small place, with a population in 1666 of only 1,500, the majority of whom were poor; 321 houses, mainly thatched, and only two new ones under construction; and a stream running down the main street which had to be crossed by stepping stones. It had a market for sheep and corn, but its main trade came from the making of malt and worsted stockings.

There seem to have been one or two large houses in the surrounding area—Charles I stayed at *Coberley Manor* in 1643, *Ashley Manor* belonged to William de Esheley in the reign of Henry III, *Boddington Manor* was said to have been a fine mansion in Alfred's time, but the one which survived the best was *Southam*, the oldest mansion in the county, which had been in the De la Beres family for many centuries. They came over with William the Conqueror and among their many distinguished descendants was one Sir Richard who rescued the Black Prince at the battle of Crecy.

Writing about Cheltenham in 1712, Sir Robert Atkins said that 'the only good seat was at Arle and the only good houses were Mr Hiet's at Alstone and Mr Mitchell's in the town'.

All this was to change when, a few years later, people began to hear about the virtues of the mineral waters. And it is then that one of the first interesting cottage names comes to light, when a mineral spring was discovered on the banks of the river Chelt near *Cold Bath Cottage*.

There is some discussion about which spring was discovered first and whether the local inhabitants already knew of the healthful properties of the waters, but when two doctors analysed the waters and declared that they possessed medicinal properties superior to any others in the entire country, Cheltenham's prosperity increased at a great rate. Visitors flocked to the town—the streets were paved and cleaned, land was purchased and houses built. Some indication of progress made can perhaps be gleaned from a book published in 1786 with the informative title of 'A Journey to Cheltenham Spa containing an Account of Cheltenham in Its Improved State'.

When in 1788 George III visited the town and stayed at *Fauconberg House* (joined a few days later by the Prince of Wales who stayed at *The Wooden House*) to go to Cheltenham became the height of fashion (and lodging fees increased from three guineas to twenty-five guineas a week!). From a mere 374 visitors in 1780, there were 1,100 in 1790, 4,000 in 1808 and 12,000 in 1836. By then great strides had been made in communications, street lighting, housing and amusements. The small Pump Room built in 1809 was replaced a few years later by a much finer one, the Imperial Spa was opened and in 1830 the superb Pittville Pump Room was opened.

The town flourished, visitors came from far and wide and some quite unusual house names (for that era) began to appear. In 1800, for example, among the more usual *Garden House, Grosvenor House, Somerset House, The Great House* (built originally as a private residence but by 1806 the largest lodging house in the town), there were *Paradise House, Milk House, Bow Window House* and the really rare *Nutshell.*

In the early part of the nineteenth century there were about 130 named properties in the town. Apart from three—*Wilkinson's Folly, Sandford Farm* and one house known as *Mrs Ironside's* —all the rest had either 'cottage', 'house', 'lodge' or 'villa' after their names—*Phoenix Cottage, Sion House, Woodbine Lodge, Cambray Villa.* Many of the names were those of towns in Britain: *Bath* accounted for two cottages, a lodge and a house; *Manchester, Warwick, Malvern* each had a cottage and a house; and others like *Chester, Derby, Nottingham* and *Richmond* had either a cottage or a house. One or two were after counties, or great families—*Dorset House, Norfolk House, Rutland Lodge, Suffolk House.*

There were *Mural Cottage* and *Miniature Cottage,* and at that time the use of surnames on houses was more popular than the present preference for Christian names—the *Smiths, Fletchers, Henneys, Fowlers, Faulkners* and *Barratts* all being commemorated, whereas *Rodney Cottage, Rollo Cottage* and *Winifred House* were among the few using forenames. Saints, however, were included: *St James' Villa, St James' Cottage, St Margarets, St George's House* and *St Julia Cottage. Jersey Villa* and *Montpellier House* were the only ones likely to be connected then with holidays, but there were many names linked with war—*Blucher Lodge, Buller House, Nelson House, Trafalgar Cottage, Waterloo Cottage, Wellington Cottage.*

Apart from *Botanic Cottage,* which is a good general name from nature and one not often seen nowadays, fruit, flowers and trees accounted for quite a few of the cottages—*Strawberry, Mulberry, Rose, Jessamine, Myrtle, Holly, Beech* and *Pine.*

By 1840 the number of 'Principal Houses and Detached Residences' had increased to nearly 200, and of these 63 had names like *Carlton House, Old Well House, Georgiana House*; 35 were Lodges of one kind or another—*Shamrock Lodge, Tarlogie Lodge, Novar Lodge,* and 24 were Villas—*Thatchley Villa,*

Blockley Villa, Greville Villa. But the interesting point here is that the word 'Lawn' was now being used—*Primrose Lawn, Painswick Lawn, Alstone Lawn, Lansdowne Lawn.* It is also apparent that people were beginning to use names which, at the time, would have been considered quite unusual—*The Aviary, The Domicile, Fancy Hall, Maisonette, Rioho Lodge, Tynte Villa.*

While local beauty spots, of which there is an endless supply in the neighbourhood, continued to provide delightful names—*Bibury Cottage, Birdlip House*—many more names from the Continent and further afield were beginning to creep in—*Tivoli Lodge, Vittoria Cottage, Mandeville, German Cottage.* There were a great many Army and Navy officers living in the town, but apart from those who saw service in India no particular pattern emerged from the house names of the others. There was an Admiral at *The Elms*, a Colonel at *South East Villa*, another at *Marle Hill*; numerous Captains at Lodges called *Oriel, Ellesmere, Sherbourne* or *Chalfont.* The Earls, Lords and Knights had an equally miscellaneous assortment—*Willoughby House, Montpellier Lodge, Claremont Lodge, Southam* and *North Lodge.*

But as time went by and new names appeared like *Fleurville* and *Maryville, Marian Villa* and *Hillside*, there also seemed to be a tendency to take the name of one house in a road and alter its ending for adjacent properties—thus in 1860 in Grosvenor Street there were *Exeter Hall, Exeter House, Exeter Lawn* and *Exeter Lodge.* Similarly in Bays Hill there were *Fauconberg House* and *Fauconberg Villa*; London Road had *Keynsham Cottage, Keynsham House, Keynsham Lawn, Keynsham Lodge, Keynsham Villa*, with *Keynsham Glen* in a side road for good measure. All most trying for the postman. Even greater confusion must have occurred in Hatherley Place and Hatherley Road which themselves contained *Little Hatherley, Hatherley Hall, Hatherley Villa* and *Hatherley Court*, with *Hatherley Lawn* in Lansdown Road.

The influence of those wealthy enough to travel, or those with overseas connections or interests, began to show quite early. In the 1830s there was a *Bahama Villa* and a *Loretto*; twenty years later *Frankfort Lodge, Italian Villa, Tyrol* and *Vallombrosa* had appeared, and by 1870 there were such continental names as *Tours Villa, Albuera Villa, Arno, Cintra, Lorraine Villa, Livorno Lodge*. Cheltenham has long been famous for its retired colonels, and there were many houses with names like *Delhi Villa, Indus Lodge, Lucknow, Sirsa House* and even *Mosquito Ghur* and *Malcolm Ghur* ('Ghur'—a house).

At the end of the nineteenth century, when other parts of the country were producing humorous names like *Updown* or *The Knock*, Cheltenham was following suit in a mild sort of way with *The Hut, Phayrecot* and *Suburban Villa*. But by 1900 it was apparent that the Lodges and Villas which once accounted for such a high proportion of names were fast giving way to the single names—*Kenmuir, Laburnum, Foxton, Kynance, Lamorna, Friarfield, Fortfield, Latimer, Kingston* and *Ewlyn*. Unusual names occurred—*Karenza, Fintray, Mockerkin, Laracor, Kilglas, Lagarie, Glevum* (from the Roman name for Gloucester). While *Eva Villa* still stood, the use of the ending '-ville' was much more popular—*Ewartville, Ethelville, Larchville, Florenceville*. There were numerous '-holmes' and '-leighs'—*Kingsholme, Langholme, Eversleigh* and *Firleigh*. Names came from all over the world—*Formosa House, Jireh House, Leiden, Normandy House*; from books—*Ivanhoe*; after important people's homes—*Farringford* where Tennyson once lived.

Amusing names continued to appear, like *Lang Syne*. One remarkable name was *Moota Moola*, the home of a Colonel. This is clearly not the slang word for money made popular by Hollywood in the 1930s—'Moola' is probably an alternative form of 'mullah', a Moslem title for someone versed in sacred law.

Ferns had become extremely popular, with various endings—*Ferncliffe, Ferndale, Fernlea, Fernhurst*: '-field' was being added to form names like *Fairfield* and *Lanesfield* and although there were still three separate *Ivy Villas* in various parts of the town,

43

Ivy Mead and *Ivy Dene* had been added.

By the 1930s the number of international names had increased enormously. More and more houses were being built, and the changes in the patterns of education, travel, communications and other influences were making themselves felt. Foreign names abounded, with more than ever from India—names that had become very familiar—*Darjeeling, Kashmir, Muttrapore, Simla, Bangalore, Delhiville, The Dak Bungalow*—all memories of years spent overseas. Not only were there reminders of India, but of countries scattered throughout the world; from Australia, New Zealand, Burma, Japan, Iraq, Egypt, Israel, Ethiopia, the USA and South America, all remembered on gates and doors by *Gaza, Fao, Ienia, Kowloon, Nizza, Nola, Olio, Osaka, Quinta, Tasmania, Tel-el-Kebir, Waihi, Arizona, Alberta, Abadan*—all the way from *Adelaide* to *Zuriel*.

This was the age when names preceded by 'The' were the choice of many—*The Barn, The Nappings, The Querns, The Thorn*. Then there were those like *The Hutch, The Niche* and *The Roost*. Names of the '*Dunromin*' type were apparent, like *Trail End* and *Dunlukin*. One sign of the times was *Tramway Lodge*, but it must not be presumed that *Wagers Court* was the precursor of a betting shop!

People then did not seem to go for mythology or superstition to any great extent, although there was one *Aquarius*. They opted for names like *Pleasant Style, Pre-Fleuri, Chosen View, Trusty Cottage, Wishmoor, Erstwhile, Mywaye, Justakot, Bon Accord*. Names that fitted into the scene were *Polo View* and *Major's Cottage*. But even then people were beginning to go for *La Casa* or *Choisi*. *Latin* is unusual, and one wonders who wished to commemorate *Zeppelin*?

Today—forty years on—do the house names of Cheltenham differ in any respect from those of other similar towns? The town has grown enormously and is much bigger than Abingdon, with a population of more than 76,000. While the visitors attracted by the mineral waters have dwindled over the years, industry brought expansion to a town which seemed once to be almost in danger from the aftermath of its dramatic rise to fame and fortune. By the middle of the twentieth century the aircraft industry had become an important feature of the town's industrial life and *Arle Court* (the 'only seat' of 1712) became both the residence and the headquarters of an important industrialist. Government offices and various light industries have been established in Cheltenham, along with the head offices of a number of companies formerly in London. With the Cotswolds on the doorstep, the town is a centre for tourism.

All this means, of course, an expansion of housing estates of all kinds, from the small semi-detached houses to the quite enormous properties in very large gardens on several of the hills above the town. But the pattern is the same as in other parts of the country —many of the houses on the new estates of smaller houses rely simply on numbers. On two developments of detached three- to four-bedroom properties, about one house in fifteen has a name. The larger houses built on land which formerly belonged to the many big mansions, or the really luxurious developments, all have names. And the names fall into practically the same pattern as elsewhere. One or two have the older types of names—*The Retreat, Greenbank, Trevose, Merryfields, Sunnybrae, Top of the Hill* and *Rosebank*: trees are as popular here as anywhere— *Tall Timbers, High Trees, Woodlands, Woodbury, Oak Magna, Willow Bend, Oakwood* and *Conkers*.

To conform with other areas Arthurian legend must appear somewhere—and it does with *Camelot* and *Avalon*. There are transferred place names—*Abingdon, St Leonards, Walton, Fritwell*, and those from other countries—*Ericeira, Thika, Malindri, Neuchatel, Karadys, Gura, The Kedai, Sulmona* and *Te Aroha*; references from literature with *Jalna, Waverley* and *Darien*; names from other languages—*Papillon, St Pierre*—names from names like *Dondor* and *The Jaynes*: jokes like *Tether's End* and *The Folly* (which bears no resemblance to the usual type of tall tower or monstrous house): the universal *Wychwood*, and the locally very popular *Windrush*.

In fact Cheltenham could be summed up by saying that although historically it is very different indeed from Abingdon, yet in its house names it follows very much the same pattern—one that may be presumed to reflect broad movements in English society and to illustrate the changing tastes of the English householder and his family over the centuries.

CHANGING TASTES

19th Century	*Between the Wars*	*Modern*
Afton Lodge	Acorns	Abyan
Aubrey House	Bybrooke	Aliz
Avonhurst	Cartref	Barbican
Bewdley Villa	Cheriton	Black Sail
Buller House	Cornerway	Casa Mia
Essex House	Green Garth	Cejunclia
Glack Villa	Grey Gables	Clamarlen
Glenthorne	Hawthornes	Dunkeld
Herbert Villa	Hilcot	Fidelis
Holly Lodge	Lymington	Hoe Hok
Laurel Cottage	Lyndene	Lelant
Monaville	Milano	Los Repones
Percy House	Mullions	Queny
Somerset Villa	Nutley	Sachigiri
Stonecroft	Pinehurst	Tara
Summerhill Lodge	Riversdale	Thika
Sunnyside	Sonning	The Ruffets
The Eyrie	The Haven	Villamil
The Grange	Upwey	Wenbans
Turret House	Wood View	Wits End

CHAPTER 5

Europe:
El Pilar, Cri-Cri, and De Groene Man

There is a certain mad-dogs-and-Englishmen feeling about the whole business of house names. This feeling grows stronger when one looks at India, with its names more English than the English, Australia, whose aboriginal place-names are now so popular in the Old Country, other parts of the Commonwealth, and the United States, where a common language and close historical links make us look for family resemblances. It is not merely the Anglo-Saxon family of nations, but the whole human family, that shares the habit of naming houses, and even some of the very same names.

Patterns of housing and the general social framework may differ between countries. Many closely-knit villages in remoter areas scarcely bother with numbers on their doors, let alone names. In the friendly huddle of old towns where houses and shops cluster together in steep streets and narrow alleys, numbers may be the only practical possibility, as with those white numbers on blue enamel which tell you where you are in a French street. But nevertheless names, and often quite extraordinary ones, are to be found throughout western Europe, and not only where people are fortunate enough to have two homes—a town apartment with a number and a seaside house with a name.

Spain and Portugal

Observation suggests that in Spain and Portugal house names are urban and suburban rather than rural, and that the display of a name on a house may go with comparative modernity and affluence. As in other Continental countries, the newer names are often in wrought-iron 'handwriting', which rarely manages to suggest the handwriting of a particular person, and can be difficult to read from the road.

In Estoril, Portugal, there are some remarkable names to be seen where there are substantial and luxurious houses belonging to royalty, aristocrats and wealthy business people, as well as more modest seaside dwellings. The smaller houses along the sea front often have girls' names. Sometimes the name exists on its own—*Rose, Mimi, Laura, Sophia, Iva, Emma, Carol, Sylvia,* and sometimes the name is preceded by 'Vivenda' (meaning home or dwelling)—*Vivenda Maria Ann, Vivenda Elena, Vivenda Isabel, Vivenda Odette, Vivenda Ester.* In some cases 'Chalet' or 'Casa' is used instead of 'Vivenda'—*Chalet Juliet, Casa Colina.* Flowers, and in particular mimosa, are very popular as names— *Casa Mimosas, Vivenda Das Rosas, Geranois, Gardenia, Casa Das Flores.*

But many house names have a religious origin, and often there will be some votive device, perhaps a lamp, frequently a picture of the Virgin Mary in wrought iron or ceramic, near the front door or on the gate post, and the house will be called something like *A Luz do Mundo, Vivenda Luzdivina, Santa Maria, Chalet S Pãola,* or *Casa de Nostra Senhora da Visitaçao.* Saints' names abound—*Santa Catarina, Santa Marta,* with *Santa Isabela* well in the lead. This is something that is very definitely not an Anglo-Saxon manifestation, but it is frequently done, with a

48

complete naturalness and simplicity.

Use is made of transferred place names in much the same way as in other parts of the world. You will find *Sagres, Casa de Nazare,* or *Provence,* near Lisbon; *Montes Claros* or *Cascais* in the Algarve; *Monchique* in the Minho—all a good many miles from the original source of the place name. The more usual types of names can be seen too—*Belvedere, Alpha, Bella Vista, Briza do Atlantico.* I hardly believed my eyes when I first saw a Portuguese version of *Mon Repos (Meu Repouso)* on the door of a very dignified home, cool and shuttered and surrounded by palm trees. Unfortunately the owners of a charming seafront villa were out, for it would have been interesting to hear the reasons for their choice of *Pin-Up,* beautifully executed on a cream ceramic plaque edged with pink and blue flowers and lit from beneath by an ornamental lamp.

There had to be a *Shangri-La,* but it was paradoxical to see a small bungalow called *Igloo* in a district where 100°F is not unusual. Nearby was *Cinderella*; a solidly built and by no means mobile dwelling called *La Roulotte (The Caravan), Dacha,* the Russian for a wooden villa in the country, and in the middle of *Pergole, Casa das Pinhas, Futuro* and *Felicidade* was the very English-sounding *Ryecotes.*

In Spain you are more likely to find names on houses in the suburbs than in villages where everyone knows where everyone else lives. In the more remote areas where there has been little social mobility there are very few names indeed, but much use is made of the blue and white metal number plate.

Instead of the Portuguese 'Vivenda', Spanish names are sometimes preceded by 'Finca', meaning property—hence *Finca Casa Nueva (The New House), Finca Tio Nelo, Finca Midda, Finca Pyalosan, Finca de Vadillo.* 'Villa' is with us once again: *Villa Virtudes, Villa Buena Ventura, Villa Luse, Villa Contenta.* Girls' names are popular—*Villa Juanita, Gloria, Meme, Anita, Keke, Villa Romona, Carmen, Villa Nancy, Villa Joana* (and this was at least eighty years old), *Margarita, Paulita* and *Anabel.*

49

D

Again, many names have religious connections, and in particular *El Pilar* is a favourite. This refers to the famous statue of Our Lady on the altar in Nuestra Señora del Pilar, a great cathedral of pilgrimage in Zaragoza. Legend relates that while St James the Great was preaching in Spain in 40 AD, a vision of the Virgin on a marble pillar supported by angels appeared before him, commanding him to build a church in her honour on that site.

Pines (*Los Pinos*), poplars (*Los Chopos*) and cedars (*Los Cedros*) appear as names, but as vast areas of the land are arid it is only to be expected that *Las Palmeras* (palm trees) put in a frequent appearance.

Along with *Mi Hogar* (My House), *Casa Encantada* (a rambling, spacious house), *Mesa Nova, Quatre Arcs, Casa Blanca,* came an unusual one—*Quinta Camarines* (a camerín is a boudoir). *El Nido* (The Nest) has a wrought iron stork on its front wall.

Some of the hotels and guest houses on the Costa Brava have English names like *Sunway, Kent House* and *Windsor.* One house near Madrid had its name in Spanish on one gatepost and in Armenian on the other. An isolated property on a main road inland had a Chinese inscription on its gates. Quite the most delightful of all was *Los Patos* (The Ducks) and there were three wrought iron ducks on the front walls and each had a name—*Julieta, Jaimito* and *Victoria.* One can forgive a good deal of wrought iron for the sake of one *Los Patos.*

House names in Spain and Portugal, where they are to be found, show variety and charm and the obvious pride and affection of the owners, as indeed do the houses themselves.

France

Contrary to any first impression that French houses are all called *Dubonnet, Byrrh* or *Brillantine Forvil,* France has an interesting variety of house names, mainly in the country, where a large board with a collection of names is often to be seen on the side of the road indicating a group of houses down a side road or perhaps hidden behind trees. Once again, names are frequently in wrought-iron writing, particularly on new houses, and quite often accompanied by a flight of wrought-iron swallows. Apart from the usual names of trees (with palms—*Les Palmiers*—very much in evidence), one of the most popular French names seems to be *Mon Rêve* or *Notre Rêve* (Our Dream), with *La Chaumière* (The Thatch) not far behind. There are, too, more humorous names than in Spain or Portugal, such as *Panique, El E Nou, Ma-Guy, Toi et Voi, Et Voilà* (which is no doubt the equivalent of the English *Tizyer*), and the now almost international *Chez Nous*, neatly inverted by one owner whose wooden plaque announced that this was *At Home*. Straightforward English names are sometimes used—*John, Villa Mary-Jack* and even *Betsy*. *Villa Mary-Jack* may almost be considered an example of Franglais.

Entirely unlike the small rural English village where most of the houses have names like *Rose Cottage, Fern Bank* or *Hill View*, the tiny French village will perhaps have one name, if any. The majority of names appear either on properties out in the country and just off the main roads, or else on the thousands of new bungalows on the outskirts of towns.

The universal word 'Villa' is often employed—*Villa Eglantine, Villa Marcelle, Villa Bleue*, and so is 'Chez'—*Chez Jean*. Occasionally one sees 'Domaine'—*Domaine Le Rond Point, Domaine Mirielle*. But apart from a few girls' names such as *Nina, Astrid* and *Odette*, most names are, of course, preceded by le, la, les, ma or mon—*La Roserae, Le Grand Champ, Les Marroniers, Mon Plaisir, Ma Chaumière*, with the feminine gender far outweighing the masculine. Flowers, trees and sunshine are much in evidence: *Edelweiss, Villa des Fleurs, L'Acacias, Le Pergola*, and *Villa Soleil*.

Sometimes a more unusual name is to be found—*Cri-Cri, Villa Poésie, Rose Mousse, Plaisance, L'Oasis, Simple Abri, May Toute, Etcha-Ona, Acco Me Play, La Détente (The Relaxation)*,

51

and again there are transferred names such as *Riviera, La Pro-vençale*, although there seems little evidence that many of these came from outside France—an occasional one like *Villa Connec-ticut*, but not many. Whereas in England there are dozens of houses called *Menton, St Malo*, or *Nice*, there are not the equiva-lent *Torquay, Bristol* or *Bournemouth* decorating French porches.

Italy

Venice has some interesting names to offer, among them *Casino Degli Spiriti*, once the meeting place of smart Venetian society. However, its subsequent history was decidedly eerie. Funeral processions had to pass the house on their way to the church of San Michele and it is supposed to have been used as a repository for corpses. Sinister tales began to circulate: there were whis-pers of smuggling. Ghosts were seen. It is long deserted by smart society, but ghostly connections still cling.

Palazzo Degli Scrigni (The Palace of the Money Chests) ac-quired its name from the rich family who once owned it. The *Palazzo Labia* was the scene of the most lavish ball of the 1950s. In earlier times its owners are alleged to have shown off their wealth at dinner parties by throwing their gold plate into the canal beneath, but being thrifty they would later have it recovered from the waters and cleaned up.

Ca' Corner ('ca' is short for casa) was famous as one of the most beautiful houses in Italy until it was completely destroyed by fire. Another house that has disappeared, this time beneath the waters of the Adriatic, is the *House of the Seven Dead Men*, a name acquired, according to the local story, through a joke that misfired. Some fishermen found a body and took it home. They told the boy who was getting their meal to wake up the 'visitor' and bring him to dinner. Worse was to come, for the obedient boy succeeded in waking the corpse, who readily presented himself at table. The seven fishermen are supposed to have died from fright.

Perhaps the most famous Italian villa dates from the middle of the sixteenth century. It is the *Villa d'Este* near Tivoli which belonged to Cardinal Ippolitto II d'Este. In its gardens is the Bernini fountain which inspired a fine piano piece by Liszt.

The *Villa Bassani,* near Sarcedo, was originally the *Villa Capra,* built by Horatio Claudius Capra, a literary man of the eighteenth century. The *Villa Eolia* is not really a villa at all but an outbuilding of a sixteenth century villa now demolished. The interesting feature here is the air tunnel connected with the nearby grottoes, which carried air of more or less the same temperature all the year round to the house.

The *Castello da Basso* (The Lower Castle), also known as *La Rocca,* in Marostica, was built in 1320, but has since been restored and added to. Now the Mayor's residence, it is famous for the ivy which climbs up the tower to a height of 30 metres.

Many of Italy's villas have changed hands and so changed their names over the years. For example, the *Villa Negri,* built in 1763 by Negri, is now *Villa Piovene*; *Villa Loschi,* erected on the site of an earlier building in 1734, and housing some of the work of Giambattista Tiepolo, is now the *Villa Zileri Dal Verme*; and the *Villa Chiericati* is now *Villa Lambert.* There are times, of course, when a villa changes its function; the Town Hall at Altavilla was once the *Villa Valmarana.*

Belgium

No one can say that the Belgians are reticent about their domestic architecture. They will build a mansion for an executive in an Antwerp suburb, put a thatched roof on it that looks as brand-new as a blonde nylon wig, and pretend the result is a country cottage. Other suburban habits like the use of names are therefore to be expected. Both French and Flemish names are found—such as *De Golven, Duinzicht, Siska, De Groene Man,*

Ons Huis, Het Zonnig Oord, which perhaps look less familiar to us than the French, many of which are common to other European countries, *Belle-Vue, Les Cygnes, Marie-José, Les Sapinières, Beau Séjour* and *Le Nid.*

A number of historic Belgian houses are connected with great painters, and three in particular with Rubens—*Veldwijk,* an early sixteenth-century moated country mansion (now a town hall); the Chateau of *Het Steen,* or *Elewijt* (first mentioned in 1304) which he rebuilt; and *Rubens House* where he died in 1640. The gardens here have been laid out exactly as depicted in one of his paintings. David Teniers the Younger lived in *De Drij Torens,* a castle-farm at Perk, and *Jordaens' House* was built by the artist in 1641 and occupied by him for nearly forty years.

Many of the old houses have royal connections. *Huis Bouchoute,* in Bruges (late fifteenth century), was the residence of Charles II of England, and Charles V of Belgium at one time occupied the *Prinsenhof,* once a burgomaster's residence, and now several hundred years later a commercial college. On the other hand, the *Maison du Roi,* in Brussels, was never actually occupied by a king, but was converted from an old bread market—*Broodhuis*—on the instructions of Charles V for the use of his officials, and it acquired its name as it was once the collecting house for taxes and rents owed to the King. Later, restored and rebuilt more than once, it became a prison, and during its chequered history it has been known by several names, including *Maison Ducale* (when it was a tax office of the Duke of Brabant), *Maison du Peuple* (in the Republican days) and now, as *Maison du Roi,* it is a museum.

Another house with a colourful past and an intriguing name is the *Castle of Gerard the Devil (Gerard Duivelsteen* or *Chateau de Gerard le Diable)* in Ghent. Originally a thirteenth-century fortress, it has in its time been a nobleman's house, an arsenal, a convent, a priests' training college, an orphanage, a reformatory and the headquarters of the fire brigade. It now houses some of the State archives.

In the fourteenth century Everard t'Serclaes was fatally wounded and died at his home, the *Maison de l'Etoile*. It was he who some years earlier, with the help of some fellow compatriots, rescued Brussels from the clutches of Louis de Male of Flanders.

The old guild houses have some fascinating names: *Maison du Renard* (the mercers' hall); *Maison de la Brouette* (grease-makers); *Maison du Cornet* (skippers); *Maison du Sac* (coopers); *Maison du Roi-D'Espagne* (bakers) and two which belonged to guilds of crossbowmen—the *Oude Handboog* and the *Jonge Handboog*. But perhaps the best is one called *Ter Buerze* whose name appears in many languages throughout the world as The Bourse, or stock exchange. This was the thirteenth-century home of the Van der Buerze family, which became an international centre of business for merchants throughout the known world.

West Germany

Although some houses in West Germany have names, for example *Waldfried, Seeblick, Alpenblick,* the practice is not as widespread as in some countries. But one or two very old houses of interest to visitors have names (some are even anglicised) that are worth mentioning. *The Samson House,* an old burgher house built in 1643, was once a wine merchant's store; the famous *Pied Piper's House* in Hamelin; *Saba Castle* where Sleeping Beauty is said to have lived; and *Sigmaringen,* a former Hohenzollern residence. In the Harz Mountains some of the old half-timbered houses, once the houses of the guilds, are still preserved: the *Brustuch,* the house of the bakers' guild, and the *Kaiserworth,* once the guild hall of the tailors, and now a hotel.

Switzerland

Not only has Switzerland any number of modern houses with names such as *Chalet Astrid, La Devinière, Les Gonnelles, Les*

Pierrettes, Le Mirador, Le Clos d'en Coulet, Villa Favorita, Les Blanchettes, Casa Peschiera, but also many whose names are associated with great figures or events from history.

Among the oldest was the fortress *Turicum* at Zurich, a Helvetian settlement which fell into Roman hands about 58BC. From the sixteenth century there are the patrician dwelling at Schaffhausen known as *Grosse Haus;* the *Hauss Zum Ritter* whose original façade painted by Tobias Stimmer in 1510 is now in a museum, and the *Schmeidstube* with its original portal and corner turret of 1653.

Gibbon has several connections with Swiss houses; he wrote 'The Decline and Fall of the Roman Empire' in the summer house in the garden of *La Grotte,* Lausanne, and saw Voltaire act in his own plays at the eighteenth-century house known as *Mon Repos,* Lausanne, now the home of the International Olympic Association—surely one of the most distinguished houses to bear this name. Voltaire himself had winter quarters for four years at *Les Delices,* Geneva, and then went to live for a short time at the *Chateau Prangins,* Lake Geneva. Later this was the home of Joseph Bonaparte. The *Villa Prangins* was occupied by ex-Emperor Charles of Austria from 1919-21, and Prince Louis Napoleon's mansion was *La Bergerie,* Lake Geneva. Wagner lived at *Villa Wesendonck,* Zurich, for a year or so, and completed 'die Meistersinger' at the *Haus Mariafeld.*

Holbein's residence is now known as *Holbeinhus,* and Byron lived and wrote part of 'Manfred' and the third canto of 'Childe Harold' in 1816 at *Villa Diodati* (which takes its name from a house no longer in existence).

Houses with more recent connections are *Maison de Verre,* built by Le Corbusier in Geneva, and *Villa Choisi,* Lake Geneva where Sir Winston Churchill spent his first post-war holiday in 1946.

EUROPE

France

Coccinelle
Chante-Bise
Clarette-Haunte
Domaine Mirielle
Jean Louis
La Croix
La Hortensia
La Roseraie
La Touche
L'Ensoleilée
Les Acacias
Villa des Hirondelles

The Netherlands

Zonzijde	(Sunnyside)
Welgelegen	(Well situated)
Nooitgedacht	(Never thought of)
Weltevrêe	(Satisfied)
Duinzicht	(Dune View)
Ons Paleis	(Our Palace)
Ons Nest	(Our Nest)
Marijke	(Girl's Name)
Parkzicht	(Park View)
Rivier en Dal	(River and Valley)
Berg en Dal	(Mountain and Valley)
Zeelust	(Sea Delight)

Spain

Amuru
El Carmen
En re Rosas
Fortuny
Los Alamos
Mati Paz
Montezumba
O'Recanto
Quinta 17 October
Saudade
Villa Felicima
Villa Inocenta

Portugal

Alatroz
Arc Luz
Casa da Portela do Rio Touro
Casa das Flores
Dinosah
Magda
Mira-tejo
Pergola
Providencia
Solar Monteiro
Solmar
Viralinho

CHAPTER 6

Britain, Australasia, India and Southern Africa - a Two-way Traffic

Around the world a remarkable amount of name borrowing goes on, to the point where one cannot always say who the original owner was. Naturally Australia, New Zealand, India and other countries have their own distinctive house names which have not so far been swapped or exported, as we shall see later in this chapter. But writing to an address on the other side of the world that begins with an English house name is a form of 'hands across the sea'.

The British have brought back memories from every country on earth. America (and in particular Iowa, Louisiana, Indiana and Wyoming) and Europe have been the source of hundreds of names. Almost every country in the world has supplied at least one name—Tibet, Ethiopia, the Galapagos Islands, Equatorial Africa and South America all provide examples. The list goes from Alaska to Japan the long way round. But the Commonwealth is one of the biggest sources of all, and the contribution of Australia is particularly notable.

In a pleasant road in Cheltenham is one of the finest examples

—a house simply called *The Strines*. From Australia we also get *Cronulla, Lithgow, Malabar, Manly, Maralinga, Mossgiel, Railton* and *Strathmore*. These are place names, but the popularity of names in the Aboriginal language is remarkable and seems to be growing, and we find *Coolangatta* (splendid view), *Carinya* (a happy, peaceful home) and *Billabong* (a pool separate from a river).

From New Zealand come *Dunedin, Waipawa, Wanganui, Rangitikei, Taranaki* and *Tokoroa*.

Earlier generations retiring from service in India brought back names like *Delhi Villa, Indus Lodge, Lucknow, Kandahar House, Kohimar, Nurlu* and *Quilon*. Some of these names are disappearing, as many of the houses were large and have offered tempting targets for redevelopment.

Other parts of the world have naturally contributed: Canada with *Ontario, Regina, Vancouver* and *Muskoko*; Malaysia with *Pasir Panjang* and *Malacca*; Pakistan with *Akora* and *Nowshera*. Borrowings outside the Commonwealth have included *Silvania* from Brazil, *Quebrada* from Ecuador, *La Paz, Tamarindo* and *Valparaiso* from other parts of South America, *Changsha, Kaoling, Kuan-Yin* and *Shanghai* from China, and *Zamalik* and *Cairo Lodge* from Egypt.

Sometimes it is impossible to say who has lent and who has borrowed. *Sharon* may be from the place-name in Afghanistan; it is more likely to be a reiteration of what became one of the most popular (and often one of the most incongruous) girl's names of the 1960s. The town of Lismore in Australia was named after Lismore in Argyllshire; there is a Ranfurley both in Alberta and in New Zealand; Tara turns up in four separate continents, and the USA has many place names that are duplicates of others throughout the world.

Australia

From the early Colonial period to the present day, Australian

59

house names have been varied in their origins. European place names appear from the first: *Grantham, Pateley, Tintern, Beaulieu House, Stratford Lodge, Eastbourne, Norwood, Como, Montpellier, Vaucluse*. Pioneers had grants of land made to them to establish cattle or sheep stations, and they built homesteads which they often named either after their families or their former homes.

One of the oldest homes is *Pewsey Vale* in South Australia, the first permanent home of Joseph Gilbert, son of the Gilberts of Pewsey Vale, Wiltshire, England. James Clinch built *Berkshire Valley* in Western Australia in 1847 on a site that reminded him of the English county in which he was born. In 1817 Thomas Archer from Hertfordshire, England, was granted 800 acres in Tasmania and built *Woolmers*, the name of an estate closely connected with his family back in England, and his brother like-wise built *Panshanger* also called after an English country seat. Captain Samuel Horton arrived in Van Diemens Land in 1823 with £1,640 of goods and cash. He was granted 1,000 acres of land on which he built a home and gave it the Lincolnshire name of *Somercotes*.

Irish castles have been the inspiration behind more than one property. *Killymoon*, Tasmania, is thought to have been built in the style of *Killymoon Castle*, County Tyrone; *Malahide*, Tasmania, was built by William Talbot, son of the Talbots of *Malahide Castle*, County Dublin.

But not all Australian house names come from place names; some are inspired by people, such as *Canning Downs*, Queensland, after the celebrated English statesman; *Elizabeth Farm House, Parramatta* (one of the oldest and most historic farm houses in Australia), was the home of an Englishman, John Mac-arthur, who emigrated in 1790 with his wife Elizabeth, and built his house with the help of convict labour. *Rouse Hill House* built in 1816 for Richard Rouse, Superintendent of Public Works at Parramatta, stands on Vinegar Hill, the scene of a battle between a party of escaped convicts and the NSW Corps in March 1804.

Thomas Laycock, the only casualty of the Rum Rebellion (and he fell down a manhole while searching Government House) built *The Retreat*, and this was later renamed *Kelvin*. John Howard Angas (son of George Fife Angas, the founder of South Australia) sent out to restore the family fortunes which had been almost wrecked by an overenthusiastic employee, married Susan Collins, and they set up home at *Collingrove*.

From literature come the universally popular *Ivanhoe*, *Raveloe* (the village in 'Silas Marner') and *Dingley Dell*. *Brickendon* is made of hand-made bricks. *Princess Royal*, South Australia, was so named because it was built on land granted to the Princess Royal Mining Company who originally intended to build a town of that name, but the mines failed and the land was sold for sheep rearing. *Rontharambo*, Victoria, stands on the end of the plains that bear the Aboriginal name. *Werribee* (from the river name meaning 'spine') built a century ago at a cost of over £60,000, was an enormous house with nearly sixty rooms, the home of a Scot who developed one of the largest pastoral empires. But perhaps one of the most attractive names is the *Humpty Doo* station in Northern Territory.

Havilah, New South Wales, named in the 1850s has an interesting story behind it. The owner of the land, Nicholas Bayly, organised a picnic with the idea of doing a little prospecting for gold, and a clergyman in the party, on finding a few specks of gold, immediately quoted from the Bible a passage referring to a river that ran out of Eden into the 'land of Havilah where there is gold' (Gen. ii); Bayly was delighted, named the property *Havilah* and subsequently built a homestead there.

Richard T. Scougall, alleged to be the first person to bring free white employees to Australia from Scotland in 1832, established himself at *Jimbour*, named from the surrounding area 'Jimba' meaning 'lush grass'. Misfortune overtook him around 1844 and he was obliged to sell out. His successor built an ornate mansion with a water pump powered by the first windmill to be erected in Queensland. Today Jimbour is a thriving community with

61

modern amenities, including an aerodrome.

The name *Cattle Chosen*, in Western Australia, explains itself. In 1832 the Bussell family moved flocks and herds up from the Flinders Bay area and settled where their animals had found good pasture. A village grew up round the homestead and the town Busselton was proclaimed in 1837. Caught trying to escape from Maria Island, the Irish rebel William O'Brien, transported in 1848, was sent to Port Arthur for greater security, where he finally made his home in *The Exile Cottage*. Visiting royalty have bestowed world-wide fame on the historic property called *Coochin-Coochin* in Queensland.

The Australian National Trust have taken over a number of historically interesting properties, among them *Como* in South Yarra, *Overland Corner Hotel*, Barmera, once a staging point on the overland stock route from the North East to Adelaide, and *Franklin House*, Tasmania, built by convict labour in 1838, renamed *The Hollies* when it was sold in 1888, but now once again known as *Franklin House* after the nearby village. *Allington*, in Berrima, was once The Victoria Inn, and a village trust set up in 1963 has set out to preserve the town as an example of early nineteenth-century colonial life in New South Wales.

Tasmania has several other house names worthy of note besides those already mentioned—*The Gardens*, St Helens, named by Lady Franklin, wife of the Governor of Tasmania, because of the profusion of wild flowers in the area; *Bridal Cottage*, Richmond, built in 1830, and *Mona Vale*, Ross, a large Victorian Italianate mansion whose designed linked it with divisions of time —365 windows, 52 rooms, 12 chimneys and 7 entrances.

Woollahra (whose aldermen were responsible for the first piece of concrete road in Sydney in 1916) is particularly keen on preserving memories of its old properties, and the names of many houses which have now disappeared have been resurrected and used to name roads in the town; for example: *Greenoaks, Mona, Kambala, Tivoli, Greycliffe, Vaucluse, Fernleigh, Wallaroy, Quambi, Lindsay, Etham* and *Eastbourne*.

Greenoaks became the residence of the Archbishop of Sydney; *The Octagon*, one of the oldest buildings erected on Darling Point (famed for its old homes) was bought in 1859 for £3,000; *Carthona*, also on Darling Point, means 'the meeting of the waters'. *Springfield* actually had a spring on its property; *Brooksby* was named after the owners' family residence in Leicestershire; *Malcolm's Folly* was begun by a sea captain named Malcolm but never finished; *Etham* was once the centre of social life; *The Willows*, built in the late 1840s, had a pond surrounded by willows in the centre of the garden, and the frontage of *Mona*, which had somehow become a rubbish dump, was the haunt of footpads and robbers who, in the mid-nineteenth century, held up carriages and attached unarmed pedestrians.

Finally there are the house names which stem from the Aboriginal language, whose growing popularity abroad has already been remarked. Here there is an almost endless source of marvellous names which not only have extremely appropriate meanings, but sound delightful at the same time: *Akora*—a dwelling; *Coryule*—hill by the sea; *Barwon*—great river; *Warrawee*—come here; *Warrock*—plenty of wood and water; *Bungarie*—a hut; *Noorong*—home; *Buninyong*—hill like a knee.

New Zealand

Although there are relatively few houses with names in New Zealand today, yet there are records of houses and other buildings with names going back long before European settlers arrived. The Maoris had sacred buildings with names like *Te Aho Tamariki* (a brilliant group of stars), *Puhikai Iti* (a small post at the top of which food is kept) near the site of the Cook Monument at Gisborne, *Te Tuahu* (sacred place) and *Whare Korero* (meeting house) on the east coast, but the most famous House of Learning called *Te Ra-wheoro* (rumbling sun) stood near Tolaga Bay. One of the largest Maori meeting houses in the country was built at the foot of Kaiti Hill, Gisborne—*Tohu-O-Rawiri* (mark or sign of David).

Many settlers from Britain took with them the custom of house naming, and so we have records of houses with names like *The Hollies*, built about 1863 for the Registrar of the Supreme Court, who planted the first holly bushes in Christchurch in his garden and thus at the same time acquired a name for his house. Along with him on the same ship went the Bishop-designate for Canterbury who apparently took one look at the plains and immediately returned to Europe by the same boat. There were extensive swamps all round, and it was easy to see how one settler's home got its name—*The Wilderness*. Dr Barker, one of the early historians of the Christchurch area, lived at first at *Studdingsail Hall*, a most apt name when all it consisted of was a tent made from the studding-sail from the 'Charlotte Jane', the ship that took him over.

Some settlers, of course, took names from their old homes, their new surroundings or from the Maori language. The Deans brothers acquired a large tract of land which they called *Morven Hills* after their old home in Scotland, but people misunderstood their pronunciation and thought they said 'Malvern Hills', and so the area acquired the name Malvern in error. The Deans called their station *Homebush*, and the surrounding bush with its variety of native bushes and trees is now preserved by the people of Canterbury. Dr Jennings, another early settler, took the Maori name for the part of the river running through Christchurch and called his house *Otakaro*.

Two suburbs of Christchurch were named from the houses of early settlers—*Linwood*, a house belonging to Joseph Brittan who went out as surgeon on the 'William Hyde' and subsequently became a member of the provincial council, and *Cashmere*, the home of Sir Cracroft Wilson the judge, who took into retirement many reminders of his days in India, including servants, donkeys, peacocks and the name. *Rosemary Cottage*, owned by a settler named Calvert, was called after Bishop Selwyn's daughter, and the home of Sir Julius von Haast, scientist, explorer, dis-

64

coverer and master-builder of Canterbury Museum, was called *Glückduf*, meaning good luck.

Larnach's Castle, the only example in New Zealand of the castle so familiar in Europe, got its name from its builder, W. J. M. Larnach. Built in 1871, it cost between £50,000 and £100,000—a large sum for those days—but in 1939 it only fetched £1,250.

Some of the historic houses are now museums, like *The Treaty House*, Waitangi, originally the home of the first British Resident. It was here that British sovereignty was proclaimed in 1840, when Maori chiefs signed the Treaty of Waitangi and acknowledged British rule in return for protection and security. Similarly, *Pompallier House*, Russell, was built for the first Roman Catholic Bishop of New Zealand, Jean Baptiste François Pompallier. So much for very early homes, apart from one more name which must be included, although strictly it belongs to a railway station. An early settler (later to become Prime Minister), on being asked to name the station said 'No, not I', and *Nonoti* it became.

New Zealanders today do not seem so keen to adorn their front doors with names, but when they do many make use of the wonderful names that have been absorbed from the Maori language —names such as *Makaraka, Pukekura, Wharenui, Matairangi, Ti Ora, Te Hiwi Marama, Mangapapa*.

Otherwise, what kind of name is chosen? Several seem to be memories of Ireland—*Leitrim Lodge, Dungannon, Wicklow, Glenmore*. Some are of the more usual English kind—*Greengables, Woodclear, Fairhaven, Morningside, Greenhill, Gateways, Willowbank* and *Dolphins. Clovelly* seems to have spread not only throughout Britain, but to Australia and New Zealand as well. To many it is a nostalgic symbol of the tiny West Country village within sound of the sea.

India

Why has the custom of house naming caught on in India to a

65

greater extent than in other parts of the former British Empire? The answer may have something to do with the survival of English as an official and business language, and with the survival of other English usages. To find English as well as Indian names on Indian homes is not so unexpected in a country where some of the formalities of the pre-war British Officers' mess can still be seen in their full splendour, and we have seen already in Chapter 4 how, in an earlier generation, English officers and colonial officials brought back Indian names to the homes to which they retired.

Although many people use numbers for their houses, there seems to be a comparatively high proportion with names. Many, of course, are of local origin, and often end in 'a', 'an' or 'am'—*Jaladrushya, Mallika, Sudhama, Kalpana, Rupayan, Shrinikethan, Anandanilayam, Santhalayam.* Some names are taken from famous places—*Vijaya* from the capital of the Forgotten Empire of Vijayanagar. The second word in a house name will often mean dwelling or house—'vilas', 'gruha', 'bhavan', 'niwas' or 'nivas', 'kutir' and 'vihar'.

Many Indian house names have special meanings: *Prasad Bhawan*—a prayer offering; *Gitanjali*—an offering of hymns; *Upanishad Vihar*—a religious text dating from about 800BC; *Meghdut*—a poem by Kàlidasa, a classical poet from Gupta times; *Uma Bhavan*—dedicated to the goddess Uma; *Seshadri*—a serpent connected with the god Uisun; *Lakshmi Vilas*—dedicated to the goddess of fortune; *Sita Niwas*—dedicated to Sita (the wife of Rama of the 'Ramayana'); *Krishna Nivas*—Krishna was a very popular god of bucolic origins; *Ratnakar*—jewelled; *Gulmohar*—a tree known as 'Flame of the Forest'; and two which follow themes very much in evidence wherever house names are to be found, those of good luck—*Kalyan Kutir,* and peace—*Shanthi Gruha,* the peaceful home.

While some houses belonging to Indians have European names and, in some cases, the kind that can be found on any English housing estate—*Mount Pleasant, Garden House, Southlands,*

Rose House, Rex Villa, Goldfinch, others, such as *Madhuban,* can also be found on houses in England. The ubiquitous *Panorama* and *Mon Repos* appear along with the *Sanctum, Dreamland, Cosy Nook* and *New Nest* variety. English place names such as *Kensington, Salisbury* and *Windsor* vie with others from overseas like *Aloha* from the USA, *Shahin* from Afghanistan, *Sita* from Tibet. *Alcazar* and *Mona Lisa* are highly individualistic, *Casa Grande* less so. *Temple View* is, however, a name one would not normally expect to find in Europe, and there are probably immediate reasons for the choice of *Himalaya.* There is even a house called *Vansittart.*

When it comes to guest houses and hotels there are many that could just as easily be found in any British seaside guide—*New Kenilworth, Happy Lodge, Belvedere, Greenlands, Pinewood, Seaview, Paradise, Sun-n-Sand* and *Marine.*

The Coronation and *Jubilee* have probably been there for a number of years, and *Kanchenjunga, Pagoda, Imperial Sable, Everest* and *Taj Mahal* are only to be expected.

Some of the palaces and temples from former times must be included. One of the most interesting is *Ankh Michauli,* which means Blind Man's Buff. It is here that the Great Emperor Akbar (a descendant of Tamerlane) is supposed to have enjoyed this pastime with ladies of his harem.

Haw Mahal, the Palace of the Winds, was built by the Maharaja Sawai Jai Singh, who gave his name to Jaipur. The medieval fort at Gwalior has within its walls *Teli-Ka-Mandir* (the oilman's temple) and *Sas-Bahu* (the mother-in-law's temple). Although *Uparkot* might at first be thought an English joke name, yet it was the stronghold of former Hindu rulers of Junagadh.

Southern Africa

While a great many people in Southern Africa use a PO box number for their address, there are far more house names in this area than one would expect, and some very unusual ones. Names from other languages, including Afrikaans, are popular: *L'Horizon, Vue de l'Est, Chez Louise, Geldenhuis, Umbalwana, Buitenzorg, Kwavullindlela, Zonnekus, Doornbult, Tjernander, Brandkop, Birds Vlei* and *Hunter's Vlei*. Many of the names follow more or less in the footsteps of house-namers the world over, with weather playing an important part: *Sun Valley, Sunridge, Sunset Place, Stormvale, Tradewinds, Westwinds, Northwind* and *Mistral*. Then there are the kinds of names you can see almost anywhere: *Farhills, Valley Gaze, High Acre, Bywood, Oatlands, Fairview, Hilldene, Glenhazel* and, of course, *Dunromin* and *Shangri-La*.

Some of the names come from Britain: *Surrey Lodge, Exeter House, Hazlemere, Headingley, Ringwood, Devon House, Savernake, Heston, Clevedon, Chipstead*—even a Welsh name, *Gwynt-y-Mor*, in a district called Llandudno.

From literature there are *Waverley* and *Camelot*, and *Bleak House* turns up yet again—strange how the most unpropitious name in all Dickens should be the one most often borrowed from him. Joint names or owners' names are by no mean rare—*Kendor, Jesland, Brooklands, Davlyn,* and there is the usual kind of joke—*Itlldo*. But some are most unusual—*Bedlam, Peacock Pie, Vagaries* and *Wide-o-Morn*. An artist's house has been called *Giotto's Hill,* and there are nautical allusions in *The Wreck, Sea Shanty* and *Quarterdeck*. And finally there are *Hazam, De Oude Molen, Paternoster, Silverboom* and *Pin Mill*.

AUSTRALASIA, INDIA AND SOUTHERN AFRICA

Australia	*New Zealand*
Avalon	Atarangi
Avoca	Awatere
Braemar	Gateways
Bunalbo	Hiwiroa
Catherineville	Karu
Coryule	Lincoln Hills
Euretta	Mapledene
Loren	Marire
Mandalay	Sevenoaks
St Ninians	Tablelands
Summerhill	Tahuna
The Gums	Windy Ridge

India	*Southern Africa*
Dreamland	Brandkop
Gulimohar	Cheriton
Rex Villa	Cobblestones
Rose House	High Noon
Rukmalaya	Hoëwinde
Sanctum	Hunter's Retreat
Seshadri	Langlea
Shardi Vilas	L'Horizon
Sita Niwas	Quarterdeck
Temple View	Sea Girt
The Cliff	Shelley Wood
The Retreat	Wychwood

CHAPTER 7

Britain and the New World

The United States of America

Like the rest of the English-speaking world, the USA is involved in a continuous interchange of names brought about by travel, trade and immigration. In England among hundreds of house names which are clearly of American origin one finds *Florida, Greenville, Indiana, Montana, Oregon, California, Cheyenne* and *Chiquita.* The hoofbeats of the ubiquitous Western seem to have thundered down a good many suburban roads in England. *Greenville* may refer to one of the main transmitters from which 'Voice of America' broadcasts can be heard by radio enthusiasts.

The United States has had its own very distinctive patterns of urban growth and architectural development. In the large, fast-growing, densely populated cities and trailing suburbs numbers are more practical than names. A terse and businesslike practicality would also be preferred by many as an expression of the American way of doing things.

Because the first part of an American house number indicates the block and the second part the actual house, addresses like 13229 Franklin Street are not uncommon.

It is not surprising that Americans visiting England for the first time experience some difficulty in finding *Silver Mist* or *Jessolo* in a village without even a street name.

In the United States today practically the only house names to be found are those on historic houses or else the big properties in the country like *Rosemont Farms, Oak Spring,* and *Winrock Farm.* Even some of the very old properties changed their names when the house changed hands; for instance, *Fawn House,* said to be one of the few remaining examples of the first houses to be built in the American colonies, was commenced around 1638 by John Fawn, a pilgrim settler. Within two years it was sold to John Whipple and became *Whipple House. The Staats House,* which survived a big fire in 1740, takes its name from its present owners; *Knoll,* so named because it stands on a bluff overlooking the Hudson River, changed hands in 1864 and was re-named *Lyndhurst.* There are houses whose names have remained the same, however. *Sagamore Hill,* once the home of Theodore Roosevelt, was named after old Sagamore Mohannis, who, as chief of his tribe, signed away the rights to the land on which the house was built. *Beauregard House,* a name of fairly recent origin, will be familiar to readers of Frances Parkinson Keyes; two of her novels deal with incidents in its history. Built by a slave dealer, it became a refuge for criminals. Confederate General Beauregard, victor of the Battle of Bull Run, had lodgings there after the Civil War, and the house is named in his memory. It was threatened by demolition at one time, but Mrs Parkinson Keyes rescued it and restored it to its former glory.

One of the houses where Washington really did sleep has been known as *Sheldon's Tavern* for more than a century. It was built in 1760 by Elisha Sheldon, but twenty years later his son turned it into a tavern. At the beginning of the nineteenth century it was renovated and has now become one of America's historic mansions.

One of Maryland's famous pioneers, Augustine Herman, settled on its eastern shore and named his house after his homeland Bohemia. But many of the gigantic houses of the present century were built by multi-millionaires: men like James Deering, a machinery salesman in Chicago who became the chief owner of the International Harvester Company. Although a bachelor, he had a sixty-nine room house built in Miami at enormous cost, and he called it *Vizcaya*. This is the Spanish version of Biscay or Biscayne, the name of one of the ships belonging to early Spanish explorers who sailed from Biscay in Spain to a harbour in Florida which they called Biscayne Bay. The Vizcaya was moored offshore from the land which Deering eventually bought for his house. But in spite of *Vizcaya's* gold bath taps, its Roman bath from Pompeii and its treasures collected from all over the world, James Deering only spent about three months a year in it. Now it is preserved as the Dade County Art Museum.

Another Florida house which attracted attention is the *Ca' D'Zan* (Venetian patois for *House of John*) in Sarasota, built like a Venetian palazzo by circus king John Ringling. Wealthy American bachelors seem to have a taste for building huge houses: the biggest in the USA is *Biltmore House,* Asheville, which cost George Washington Vanderbilt almost one and three-quarter million dollars. Its name comes from a combination of 'Bildt', a town in the Netherlands from which the family originally came, plus 'more', an English word for rolling, upland country. But California's *La Cuesta Encantada* must be one of the world's most expensive houses. It cost William Randolph Hearst more than thirty million dollars. Houses like this provided Orson Welles with the inspiration for *Xanadu* in 'Citizen Kane'.

By comparison *Ramsbury Manor,* which fetched Britain's record price of over half a million pounds a few years ago, went more or less for a song.

The West Indies, the Caribbean, Bermuda and the Bahamas

If names are uncommon in the USA, there is an ample supply not far away.

In the Caribbean, English-type house names abound, often on the houses of people educated in the UK, and names such as *Glencoe, Hatfield House, Trent House, Byways* and even *Mon Repos* are quite a familiar sight.

In Puerto Rico, Guyana and Jamaica modern names come from a variety of languages, but much the same pattern appears to have been followed as can be seen elsewhere in the world. There are transferred place names—*Madrid, Florida, New York, Inglaterra, San Sebastian, Elba*; ones with distinct English connections—*Oxford, Penzance* and *Ventnor*; the type that can be found throughout the world—*Oaklands, Stonehaven, The Homestead, The Anchorage, Bracken Hill, The Orchard* and *The Cedars*; names based on personal names—*Cynthue* which belongs to Cynthia and Hugh, and *Scotland*, the home of the Scots. Some concern the weather—*Sunridge, Ocean Breeze, White Clouds* and *Trade Winds*; and some come from literature—*Casa Cervantes* and *Dunsinane*. There are names from several languages —*El Arco Iris, La Concha, La Posada, Hogar, Hacienda Roses, La Siesta, Maison Blanche, Pierre, Normandie* and *Casa Blanca*; references to the past—*El Conquistador*; to folklore—*Fairymeade*; and to the future—*Infinity* and *Flying Saucer*—they are all to be found.

In the Bahamas there are *La Feuillie* (The Leafy Retreat); *Portree* named after the owners' home on the Isle of Skye; *The Columns*, so called on account of its balcony supported by columns, and *Journey's End*.

But for marvellous names like *Sally's Fancy* and *Anna's Hope* one must turn to the old sugar plantations of Guyana and the Virgin Islands. Who could help recalling the romance, and perhaps the heartache, evoked by such names as *Upper Love, Lower Love* and *Jealousy*, with *Bachelor's Adventure* adjacent to *Maiden's Despair*? Although many of the old narrow strips of plantations have been grouped together to form large units, each strip still retains the name it was given by its original owner. The origins of many of the names are buried in history, but it is easy

73

to visualise what lay behind such choices as *Mary's Hope, Paradise, Good Hope, Content, Two Friends, Vreed-end-Hope* (meaning Peace and Hope), *Werk-en-Rust* (Work and Rest) and *Endeavour*. On the other hand *Meer Zong* (More Sorrow) and *Glazier's Lust* convey a rather different impression.

Some of these old houses have featured in books and films— *Farley Hill*, Barbados, was partially restored to appear in the film 'Island in the Sun', and *Rose Hall*, once one of the finest great houses in Jamaica, with its 365 windows, 52 doors and 12 staircases, home of Mrs Rose Palmer, was featured in the novel 'The White Witch of Rose Hall', although legend seems to have mixed up Rose with her sister Ann, who was supposed to have been the white witch.

Sam Lord's Castle on the coast of Barbados, now a luxury hotel, has its own tale to tell. In the days before ships were equipped with modern navigational aids, they sometimes mistook the lights hung on palm trees in the garden for the lights of ships safely at anchor. When they foundered on the dangerous reefs nearby Sam Lord was there to salvage the cargoes from the wrecks.

Of the houses with historical connections, perhaps *Judith's Fancy* has one of the most attractive names. Overlooking the Cape where Columbus anchored in 1493, it was the residence of the Governor of the Knights of Malta. *La Fortaleza* (the Portuguese name for a fort, also denoting fortitude and courage) has been the seat of Puerto Rico's government for over four hundred years. This name is also found in other parts of the world. On an island in the river Mazaruni lie the ruins of the Dutch fort of *Kijk-over-Al* (Look over all), the seat of the Dutch government in the seventeenth century, and the Colony House built in the early eighteenth century in Surinam was called *Huis Nabij* (House Nearby) as it was built near a fort at the mouth of a river.

One of the oldest houses still standing in this part of the world is *Casa del Cordón* (The House of the Cord) so named because of the stone carving of a monk's girdle above its doorway. It was built in the early sixteenth century and Diego Columbus lived in it for a time.

Tucker House, Bermuda, was named after Bermuda's Colonial Secretary during the American Revolution. It was famous as the home of a slave who escaped from the South and after many adventures became a member of the House of Representatives. A little cottage named *The Old Rectory* (although it is not clear how it got this name) was renovated in 1703 by a pirate named George Drew and subsequently he too became a pillar of the community.

We have traced the borrowings, exchanges and original names across a large part of the English-speaking world. As a rest from these wanderings we may now turn to *Dunromin.*

THE NEW WORLD

Blue Shadows
Buena Vista
Carlton
Cascadilla
Fort Belle
Harold's Hill
Havagash
La Feuillie
LBJ Ranch
Monymusk
Oaklands
Oak Spring

Penzance
The Anchorage
The Cedars
The White House
Roodal's Residence
Roundway
Vauxhall
Ventnor
Vista al Mar
Whitehall
Windhaven
Winrock

CHAPTER 8

Dunromin

This is the place to salute all those who from necessity or inclination have made moving house their main hobby in life. Their house names often express obscure longings, forebodings, hopes or superstitions. They may, on the other hand, express nothing at all as in the case of one of our family who moved fourteen times between 1879 and 1957. Strictly speaking he need never have moved at all as *Glendare,* the house where he was born, was practically on the premises of his family business. But he liked moving and after *Glendare* he lived successively in *Goodrington, The Hill House, Rostrevor, Wayneflete* (which he immediately re-named *Coombe House*), *Pinewood, Benvuela, The Woodlands, Orchard Cottage, Riding Barn, Crossacres* and *Redmarley* (which incidentally is nothing to do with the colour, but means open land near a reedy lake). For two of his houses he was content with plain numbers. Generally he accepted the names he found and only once did he dislike a name so much that he altered it. And nobody ever prevailed on him to announce to his friends and relatives that the time had come to give up his favourite sport: so no house of his ever attempted to placate the family, or the Fates, with a name like *Dunromin*. It was a name he quoted with derision. *Dunromin, Dunrovin* and their derivatives have been much used over the last forty years or more. Fifty years ago there was a *Dunlukin* and there is at least one *Dunhuntin* today, but these do not seem to have the popularity of the other two.

Such a name could be a declaration of intent, a piece of wishful thinking, or an announcement that the family had come home from abroad or finally made up its mind about its chosen mode of life. The classical version is *Ithaca,* to which Ulysses returned after all his wanderings and adventures. *Settledown, Contental, Everhome, Trail End, Moorings* and *The Haven* all express this idea which is, after all, part of what we mean by 'home', and hence something we would expect to find expressed in many ways, sometimes with style and originality as in *Timelock* and *Gone to Ground.*

Some prefer not to tempt Providence and adopt what they hope will prove to have been a cautious understatement— *Erstwhile, Interlude, Rest-a-Whyle, La Siesta, Pas sans Peine,* and the more unabashed *Forty Winks.*

As with boats and racehorses, a name may have an almost magical power for good or evil, and the choice of a name of good omen recurs again and again in different forms. *Deep Roots, Journey's End, Serenity, The Leisure, Peaceful Home, Tranquillity, Quiet Ways, Resting* and *Nestledown* all express this idea of home.

It is possible to discern in the recent development of names like these a shift in emphasis from family names and pride of property toward autobiography and the expression of the owner's personality, tastes or humour. So one finds autobiographical names like *Admiral's Rest* and hopeful names like *Happy Days, Happy Landings, Halcyon, Gai Séjour, Sans Larmes, Joylands, Merryways, Merrythought* and *Merrie Mead.* To inhabit something called *Merrie Mead* year in, year out, through hail, slush, snow and inflation might be to regret the desperate cheerfulness of the name. Some such names become too much like a permanently fixed grin. There are therefore the subtler psychologists who have read of the attraction of opposites, and who produce names like *Hangovers, Gossips, Quarrels Copse* or *The Last Straw*.

When the ultimate goal has been reached and *Dunromin* or its equivalent stands before the weary traveller, the effect is sometimes one of inarticulate anti-climax: it is noticeable that some people who have achieved their ambition to retire to the sea promptly call their houses *Cockfosters, Wakefield, Edgware* or *Ilford*. But incongruous though it may seem to have a sparkling white house overlooking the bay and call it after a northern industrial town, this may provide the owners with a permanent reminder of old friends and jobs that enabled them finally to retire to a house by the sea, or of family ties with their former home town. Retirement may be the goal, but the serenity and wisdom of advancing years are not always taken very seriously—the ages of man run, not very respectfully, from *Salad Days* via *Agecroft* to *Doddering Heights*, which has, however, a certain defiant the-best-is-yet-to-be ring about it.

On England's south coast—an area much sought after for retirement—can be seen names like *Sydenham, Bedford, Didcot, Durham, Rothwell, Hainault, Perivale, Stafford, Oban* and *Cheam*. (Did the owners of *Cum Hardy* come from Chorlton?)

Some of these reminders will be of remote places because many people nowadays work in foreign countries building dams, bridges and power stations, manning oil refineries, undertaking scientific surveys, cultivating and manufacturing in hitherto uninhabited places—in fact living and working in places totally unimagined a few decades ago. This can be seen in the number of references to the oilfields of the world: *Abadan House, Kuwait Cottage, Alwand, Karun, Qara Su, Paulo Seco* and *Gach Saran*.

People who have spent their lives travelling quite often go for unusual place names such as *El Mersiah* from the Sahara, *Bunda* from the Congo, *Corrientes* from the Argentine and *Dampak* from Java: all to be seen in the British Isles.

The idea of using transferred names is not, of course, prac-
tised only by those who have retired to a different part of the
country. Not only in Britain but throughout the world gateposts
and doors bear legends of places hundreds of miles away:
thus *Burton* turns up in Southsea, *Croydon* can be found deep
in the heart of the Oxfordshire countryside, *Farnborough* in the
Isle of Wight, *Paignton* in Lancashire, *Provence* in Portugal,
Windsor in Sitges, *Berkshire* in Australia, *Wicklow* in New
Zealand, *Portree* in the Bahamas and *Lands End* in India.

And beyond *Eldorado* or *Shangri-La* there is a region of mental emptiness well described by William Empson:

> The more things happen to you the more you can't
> Tell or even remember what they were.

This is the limbo of semi-names and non-names like *Sumware,
Itlldo, Tizyer, Hereami, Fokia,* or at the final extreme *Wedunno,
Noname* or *Innominatum.*

Good fortune and ships coming home: luck and money. Jokes
about money: will they be enough to frighten the wolf from the
door? In some quarters mention of money might at one time have
been considered bad form. Any such taboos must have greatly
weakened. There may be self-satisfaction, as in *Costa Plenti,
Justinuff, Paide, Title Deeds* and, (brother to *Dunromin*) *Dun-
owen,* but though much of the magnificence of the past rested on
shaky financial foundations or came from questionable origins
(think of Nero's *Golden House*), it has been left to the present
age to proclaim, with names like *Langloan, Pennycuik, En
Rouge* and *Longwaite,* a poverty at once financial and linguistic.

Names which are simply derived from coinage are rather a
different matter and some of them at least have a certain charm.
Pennies are the most popular: *Pennies, Pennytale, Pennygate,
Pennystone, Pennyroyal,* but *Halfpennies* and a *Threepenny Bit*
also occur, and the number in a particular family may be indi-
cated by *Four Farthings* until more farthings arrive. The antique

79

and decorative associations of old coins are recalled by *Ducats* and *Florins*.

But whatever the formulae, one's door and one's roof tree must be protected from evil influences, while friendly powers are summoned to keep watch. Both in house building and in house naming, superstition—and sometimes ceremony—have played their part through the ages, and they still do.

In England there is little evidence to support the fact that actual ceremonies are carried out in England on the completion of a building, apart from the 'topping out' ceremony, which sometimes takes place on the completion of the outer structure of a particularly large building. Then a representative of the organisation for which the development is taking place is invited to put in the last shovelfuls of concrete, flags are flown and toasts are drunk on the roof from a barrel of beer specially taken up for the purpose.

Throughout France and Spain though, fir trees, branches or flags can frequently be seen fixed on to a gable end or roof of a house under construction. At one time a fruit tree (for fruitfulness) was fixed to the chimney stack. In medieval times the land for the building had to be consecrated and the day and the hour auspicious. Local spirits and earth spirits had to be driven away and witches' spells destroyed.

Occasionally today certain common articles, perhaps a newspaper as well, will be incorporated in the foundations of a new building, but this is merely for the enlightenment of future archaeologists. At one time omens of good luck had to be placed in the foundations—bread, salt, herbs, and money. Children were once sacrificed and their bodies incorporated into the walls of castles and houses, since it was believed that the foundations must be laid in blood if they were to survive for any length of time. Substitutes in the form of fowls, cocks, coffins, images and dolls are said to have been found in old houses and churches. But not all rituals took such hair-raising forms. In some parts of the world in early times workmen were feasted and entertained during building operations, and dances were held when the job was finished.

Inscriptions both inside and outside the home have been common practice throughout the world, from 'God Bless Our Home' on the fanlight to sacred Eastern texts to repel evil and bring good luck. In some countries a set of horns placed on the floor was thought to ward off the evil eye, and a house leek growing on a roof has been a sign of good luck for many generations (and at one time it was credited with discouraging witches and fevers too!).

Although the fir tree has, since very early times, been of particular significance in protecting a house from evil, yet today *The Firs* and its derivatives are not nearly as popular as names based on other trees such as oaks or pines. The story behind *Image House*, a cottage in Cheshire, strongly suggests the belief held in many parts of the primitive world that if you wished evil on a person you had only to make an image of him and stick pins into it and the person would die. The house contains a number of stone heads said to be like the court officials who sentenced a poacher to several years' transportation for killing a gamekeeper. On his return, the poacher tried to get his own back by carving and cursing the heads. No one knows whether he was successful, but at least it gave an interesting, although somewhat macabre, name to the property which has lingered on for well over a century.

There are a great many names with a superstitious origin on modern houses. Puck, a mischievous household spirit of English folklore is responsible for quite a number: *Puck House, Puck Hill, Pucklands, Puck's Thatch,* even *Puck's Paigles* ('paigle' meaning a cowslip). The medieval English 'pouke' was a rather different character and often identified with the devil.

The name *Bogeys* is rather a curious choice, since a bogey is said to be a terrifying spirit of uncertain, but probably hobgoblinish, nature. Although the word 'bogey' is a nineteenth-century word, it may have derived from the medieval English 'bogge' or

81

F

'bugge', meaning terror and bugbear. The bogey-man is sometimes used to frighten children: does it now serve to put off unwelcome callers? But if *Bogeys* is rather off-putting, what about *Bunyip*, said to be a bellowing water monster of Australian native mythology who lives at the bottom of lakes and water holes into which he draws his human victims, and *Gremlin*, a relatively modern addition to the spirit world? The latter was first seen during World War I, although nobody would admit to it for several years. This demon appears to pilots and aircrews and usually causes a lot of trouble, although some credit it with bringing airmen back to safety in impossibly damaged planes.

Witches, *Witches Moon* and *Broomsticks* show that the old lady with the tall hat and the black cat hasn't yet been forgotten, and *Covenstones* may once have been the site of an alleged witches' coven.

Another name acts as a charm and guards against witchcraft and all kinds of dangers. This is *Amulet*, and not only does it give protection to the wearer, but it brings good luck as well. Yet another house is called *The Mascot*, which is a person or thing supposed to bring good luck to a household. One of the most magical plants of European folklore is remembered in *Mistletoe*. Faith in its mysterious powers has been widespread for many centuries. A mistletoe rod cut on Midsummer Eve will indicate buried treasure; mistletoe needs no key to open locked doors; hung over doorways it prevents the entrance of witches. *Candles* have been used from ancient times in rituals. In folklore much can be read in the way a candle flame burns.

Mischievous spirits abound and magic is abroad, but obviously ghosts are not welcome. There is one house near a churchyard named *Spooks* and one called *The Haunt*, but this could just as well be the convivial variety rather than the supernatural. Goblins, elves, dwarfs, pixies and gnomes exist in abundance and sometimes are also visible, small as life, in plastic in the garden. *Goblins* and *Goblins Glade* will have a rather unstable life, since goblins are supposed to be domestically helpful, but also bad-tempered and destructive. *Gnomes Cottage, Elf-lands* and *Leprechaun's Leap* all offer their saucers of milk to the little folk. In advanced forms of this condition, the gnome-addict breaks out in staggering displays of virtuosity with plastic toadstools, artificial logs and red waterwheels.

The Dragon House and *Dragon's Spinney* have a somewhat forbidding ring, yet in spite of the fact that dragons must be propitiated by human sacrifice, people all over the world love stories about them, incorporate them in textile designs, and now include them in house names.

The Wish is clearly the dream-come-true of its owners, and whoever lives at *Wishing Well* has no doubt had some experience of the many wells and fountains that are said to grant your wish if you throw a coin into the water.

The crock of gold appears again at *Rainbow's End.*

Two names signifying good luck are *Horseshoes* and *Horseshoe Ridge.* A horseshoe over the door is protection against evil, but it must point upwards so that the good luck will not run out. Its magic powers might come from the fact that it is made from iron—a repellent to witches and evil spirits.

The border line between magic and religion is marked by one beautiful name with a double meaning—*Touchwood*: the house stands at the edge of a wood, and we touch wood (or say 'touch wood') to avoid calamity or express some special hope. It is better if the wood comes from the oak or a similarly sacred tree; sometimes the gesture has been interpreted as an appeal to the protection of the Cross. The name has that quality of seeming right at first glance, instinctively appropriate.

Hopes and superstitions lead by a natural process of evolution through magic and ritual towards religion. The religious impulse may be more or less traditional, primitive and unreflective, or conscious and deliberate, and may go back to something very deep in collective experience.

The need for the Jewish race to set an identifying mark on their houses goes back to the Old Testament and is commemorated in the Feast of the Passover. *Mizpah* is more often found engraved inside a ring given as a love token than on a front door, but it comes from Genesis xxxi, and was one of the names of the pillar and heap of stones put up by Jacob and his brethren in the mountain of Gilead.

> '... Laban said "This heap is a witness between you and me today". Therefore he named it Galeed, and the pillar Mizpah, for he said, "The Lord watch between you and me, when we are absent one from the other".'

Nirvana is the final state to which the Buddhist aspires. This is perhaps what *Nirvana* owners really mean, rather than 'release from life, extinction and annihilation'. Several houses have Biblical geographical references—*Elim*, a station in the wanderings of the Israelites, noted for its fountains; *Emmaeus House*, after the village near Jerusalem to which the two disciples were going when Jesus appeared to them after His resurrection, and *Salem*, both the former name for Jerusalem and also the country of King Melchizedek.

Do those who have chosen *Loreto*, after the Italian town, know the legend of the angels who carried the shrine of the Virgin to the Church of the Holy House in 1294, thus making it a place of pilgrimage? *Shamrock*, the national emblem of Ireland, has a religious significance too. St Patrick, the patron saint of Ireland, supposedly used its leaf pattern to illustrate the Trinity. *Aquila* recalls not only the Northern constellation in the Milky Way, but also Aquila the tentmaker, a great friend of St Paul.

Associations with religious places are still cherished where they occur. Many properties on land once owned by the Abbeys still commemorate their former inhabitants—*Monkspath, Monkwood, Friarsfield, Whitefriars, Abbotstone, Abbotswell, Abbeymead, Abbey House, Monk's Cottage* in Priests Lane, *The Old Priest House* (of which there are still many in existence); and where the Church owns (or owned) land, there are many like *Church Cottage, Church End* or *Bishop's Orchard*.

The lure of strange gods and ancient cults remains very strong, and as a result examples of *Druids Cottage* and *Stonehenge* can be found scattered all over the country, often many miles from the actual site on Salisbury Plain of the great stone circle. If there are picturesqueness and Gothic mystery at one extreme, there can be religiosity or simple piety at the other, with *The Rosary*, *Shrove Cottage*, *The Cloisters*, *The Sanctuary* and *Vespers*.

Our examples have ranged from semi-articulate wishes for good fortune to the deliberate invocation of supernatural powers. In this latter category saints' names are of particular interest. The idea of a patron saint goes back at least to the Middle Ages and many of the favourite patron saints are still to be found, as well as some unexpected ones. As far back as 1658 there are records of a house in Oxford named after *St Katherine* (now appealed to by spinsters in search of a husband). Later there were *St Ann's Cottage*, *St George's House*, *St James' Villa*, and one of the early examples in Torquay was a house called *St Elmo*, after the patron saint of Mediterranean sailors. All the *St Patrick's* are dedicated to the patron saint of Ireland, who also looks after sailors.

A number of houses bear *St Ninian's* name. He evangelised the Northern Britons and Picts. Those 'of sound common sense, sane good humour and generous ideals' have chosen *St Theresa's* or *St Teresa's*.

St Nicholas is a favourite. Apart from his associations with Santa Claus and the custom of giving gifts, he is also regarded as the patron saint of children.

St Edmund's House might be after any one of five; four of whom were hanged, drawn and quartered. *St Jude*, perhaps better known for his frequent appearances in the personal columns of The Times, was the brother of St James the Less. *St Hilda's* is after the saint who exercised much influence in the early Church.

St Michael's commemorates the patron saint of policemen, *St Adrian's* the patron saint of soldiers and butchers, and *St Botolph's* one of the foremost missionaries of the seventh century.

With these noble figures, it is perhaps fitting to end this chapter in which the endeavour has been made to trace a common impulse from its most everyday and banal forms, through crossed fingers and uneasy jokes, to the traditional piety which figures in house names all over the world to this day.

DUNROMIN

Bonne Nuit
Dreemlang
Eureka
Far Crye
Gay Heritage
Gay Times
Halcyon Days
Happy Days
Hermit Hill
Hi Hopes
Home Haven
Hopecroft
Journey's End
Joyville
Merrythought
Pax
Peacehaven
Peace and Plenty
Que Sera
Quiet Hills
Searches End

Seldom Seen
Serene
The Rest
Touchdown
Trips End
Why Worry

Costa Plenti
Five Farthings
Halfpenny Furze
Penny Broom
Penny Cottage
Windfall

Abbey Cottage
Church View
Greyfriars
St Barnabas
St Benedict's
St Clement's
St Crispin's
St Mary's
St Oswald's

CHAPTER 9

Mobile Homes, Flats and Holiday Memories

It was a Frenchman who said that nothing is as permanent as the temporary. There are interludes in people's lives which they may have good reason for commemorating with a name, even if their home was a temporary one. Messing about in boats or going to the seaside (or living there) can open up a world very different from the smug conventions of villadom. And the places of first meetings or honeymoons are a natural thing to remember.

Housing shortages have led to the development of a special type of large luxury caravan which can be towed to a permanent site. Whether or not people intend to live there for ever, they often give names to their homes. Some of these show the pleasure of the owners in having a place of their own—*At Last* or *The Haven*; some choose more usual names—*Shangri-La, The Channings, Inglenook* or *Magpie,* but there are a number of surprises, including *Ur of Chaldeans.*

The Victorians predicted that in the year 2000 there would be mobile homes—complete with names of course. One illustration in 'The Nineteenth Century' shows a caravan called *Villa*

Beauséjour being driven around the countryside, complete with roof garden.

Home to another rather special section of the community at the turn of the century was a narrow boat. These boats plied up and down the waterways, carying cargoes of coal, corn, limestone, bones, gas tar and manure. Their names are so delightful that no apology is needed for including them here. Although girls' names were very popular indeed in the 1880s, they were by no means the only type of name used—moral uplift also makes its appearance: *Perseverance, Good Intent, Mean Well, Live and Let Live, Guide Me Right, Industry* and *Economy.* Names like *Powerful, Early Bird, Warrior* and *Forward* show the faith the boat people had in their craft, although some owners must have been somewhat discouraged when they called their boats *Road to Ruin* and *What Next.*

Some names came from overseas: *Madras, Bombay, Parramatta, Africa, Sydney, Rotterdam* and *Quebec,* and Irish patriotism crept in with *Shamrock.*

But the old-fashioned Christian names used make fascinating reading. In 1880 there were *Annie, Fanny, Minnie, Nellie, Sarah-Ann, Amelia, Mary-Ann, Rose-Ellen, Sophia* and *Mary-Jane,* and on the boys' side *Clarence, Alfred* and *Bertie.* By 1917 the list had changed somewhat and now included *Freda, Hilda, Beatrice* and *Lottie.* By 1925 *Tom, Len, Edward* and *Reggie* sailed alongside *Polly, Aileen, Lucy, Gwendoline, Grace, Flora, Clarice* and *Lily.* Just before World War II there were *Charmian, Peggy, Pearl, Girl Pat, Mavis, Muriel, Vera, Joyce* and *Shirley.* By now boys' names had changed too, with *Robin, Tony, Bob, Fred, Phil* and *Mac* appearing on the waterways. The wars had an effect on the boats' names too: in the early days they were called *Admiral Jellicoe, General Buller, Lord Kitchener, Waterloo, Ladysmith, Somme* and *Hardy,* and during World War II *Montgomery, Commando, Wavell* and *Tripoli* appeared. Other national events also had their effect, and particularly in the 1930s, with *Queen Mary, Jubilee, Edward VIII, Coronation* and *Mrs*

Simpson, and years later, more ominously, *Atom.*

Today there are very few narrow boats left, and only the motorised ones have families living aboard. What of their names? More place-names seem to have crept in—*Stamford, Tadworth, Effingham*; fish are as popular as ever—*Trout, Tench, Shad*; *Jupiter, Saturn* and *Aquarius* still glide by and leaders like *Mountbatten* are remembered, but it is sad that soon there will be very few boats left with their gaily painted sides and such proud names as *Courageous, Endeavour, Gladiator, Worcestershire Lass, The President, Emperor* or *Providence.*

There is a liveliness about the names of temporary homes that makes many of them especially attractive: it is as if they could afford to be just so much more outrageous.

Blocks of flats

Another kind of population movement has required civic authorities, rather than individual owners, to choose names. Slum clearance on a massive scale has led to the building of high-rise flats—communities in themselves, and in many big cities each tower block has its individual name. The names are chosen in a variety of ways: sometimes after civic dignitaries (e.g. *Royce Court* after Sir Frederick Royce); sometimes after well-known local geographical features, or perhaps even after an important local industry such as *Lincoln Court* and *Shackleton Court*, Manchester, after aircraft manufactured by A. V. Roe.

The story behind *Fletcher Court* and *Hambrook Court* in the London Borough of Camden is an interesting one: an unexploded bomb was found nearby, and defused by the Army's Bomb Disposal Squad; later the Borough Council very fittingly decided to name two blocks of dwellings after the soldiers concerned.

The idea of naming a block of dwellings after a benefactor is, of course, not new. There are a number of *Peabody Buildings* and *Peabody Estates* in London named after the American financier George Peabody, a philanthropist who not only saved the state of Maryland from bankruptcy in 1835, but gave $2\frac{1}{2}$ million to the City of London for the construction of low rental working-men's tenements.

The word 'towers' has become fashionable for high-rise flats: Leeds has *Boston Towers, Carlton Towers, Grantham Towers*; Southampton has chosen to name some of its tower blocks after big cities of the world—*Rotterdam Towers, Canberra Towers, Oslo Towers*; Liverpool chooses both *Tower* and *Heights*—*Windsor Tower, Belem Tower* (after the famous landmark at the entrance to Lisbon harbour), and *John F. Kennedy Heights*; Victoria, Australia has its 30-storey *Park Towers*.

Housing authorities often choose names in particular categories: Liverpool has a series of famous people—*Attlee House, Churchill House, Eden House, Garibaldi House, Macmillan House;* Birmingham has *Wordsworth House, Browning Towers, Cavell House, Nuffield House, Wells Towers,* and battles are recalled with *Naseby House* and *Inkerman House*; Bristol looks to history for *Armada House*.

Whatever method is used, whether it is *Cité Radieuse*, an enormous development full of large windows and balconies built by Le Corbusier on the outskirts of Marseilles; *Cosmopolis* (from the Greek 'world city'), *Lands End* and *St James' Court* in India, or *Coronation Court* in Liverpool, each flat must have a number as well, but at least a meaningful name gives each block some individuality.

Boarding houses then and now

The Ritz, The Palace, The Ambassador, The Grand—we can find names like these in hotels around the world. A century ago most people who couldn't afford full board rented apartments, took their own food and were charged for the use of the rooms, the landlady's services in cooking the food they handed to her each day, and 'the cruet'. Blackpool and Morecambe were famous for their rows of terraced boarding houses with spotless lace curtains, whitened front steps and shining brass door knockers.

In the middle of the nineteenth century many boarding houses were known simply by numbers—17 Lower Rock Gardens, 105 Marine Parade—but a hundred years ago you could have stayed in Blackpool at such establishments as *Leamington House* or *Princess Villa*. Had you been particularly concerned for your health you might have stayed at *Bath Cottage*, Hygiene Terrace. In Brighton you might have chosen one of the several mansions, such as *Lion Mansion, Cavendish Mansion, Bellevue Mansion* or *Belvedere Mansion*.

By 1930 'lodging houses' were giving place to guest houses and private hotels. 'Cottage' and 'villa' had disappeared entirely and been replaced with single names such as *Bryncliffe, Claremont, Ingledene, Seacliffe, Acristo, Moorings*. Occasionally 'mansion' still appeared—*Palace Pier Mansion, Argyle Mansion,* but more owners were referring to their establishments as *The Lyric, The Manor, The Dudley,* or *Aqua Private Hotel, Highclere Private Hotel, Exeter Private Hotel, Homelands Private Hotel*.

Some chose prestige names like *Sandringham, Balmoral, Windsor, Blenheim*; others used transferred place names—for example on the south coast were *St Ives, Northumberland Hall, Haslemere, Lincoln House*. Continental names had already begun to creep in, although not to the same extent as today—an occasional *Menton, Trouville, Chez Nous* or *Mon Abri*. But a lot of emphasis was placed on names suggesting sun, sand, cliffs and the sea—*Sunny Cliff, Sandilands, The Beach, The Cliffs, Marine Hotel*.

Today, however, names of guest (not boarding) houses and private hotels come from all over the world and the influence of television with its travel documentaries, and the opportunities for owners and guests to travel abroad have led to a very wide variety of names. Blackpool offers *Toledo, San Remo, Sorrento* or *Vancouver*. Morecambe proprietors have gone all the way from nearby *Bolton* to *Stresa, Capri* and *Montserrat* in their search. Not that the older types of names have been abandoned entirely. You will always find *The Channings, The Chimes, Strathmore, Sandringham, Regency House, Cavendish, The Berkeley, Glenside* and others that have been in vogue for many years.

The further south you go the more cosmopolitan the names become. In Torquay alongside *Majorca* and *Casa Torina* are *Australia, Melbourne, Adelaide, Bermuda, Toorak, Kotri, Timaru* and *Kuling*. The *Chez Nous* and *Shangri La* of yesterday are the *Bienvenue, Hacienda, Mañana* or *Casa Nova* of today. Further along the coast it is even more romantic—*The Orient, Barbary, Kantara, Elsinore* and *Medina*.

There has always been an underlying feeling that a name connected with royalty or the aristocracy will bring the customers pouring in; as well as *Windsor* and *Sandringham,* there are thousands of small hotels called *The Royal, The Prince, The Princess, The Baron, Earl Mount,* or *Osborne House.*

The naming of guest-houses and small hotels follows the modern pattern of naming private houses, and uses many of the same sources: famous people from *Homer, Ruskin* and *Bronte* to *Novello* and *Ellington*; characters from literature like *Sinbad* and *Sherlock*; joint names such as *Ken-Ray, Dorvic, Thelma-Lyn, Carol-Ann.* A guest house must have a distinctive name to attract the customer and in the more far-fetched names the pressures of competition can be felt.

The jokes try to persuade the guest to stay in a quiet, relaxed atmosphere—*Linga Longa, Staymor, Peace and Plenty, To-Rest-In, Interlude, Goodrest* and *The Roost,* alongside *Welcomin, Yeoldun,* and the now much tried *Idonow.*

Holiday memories

Among holiday souvenirs are names—names of ships and names of places. For some people the most romantic associations are with the great passenger liners. It would be awkward to call a house by the name of one of the big Queen liners, but others that regularly appear are *Chusan, Arcadia, La Normandie, Oronsay, Franconia* and *Devonia.*

Changing fashions in the use of names from holiday resorts provide a revealing marginal comment on the social history of the last hundred and fifty years.

In the early ninetenth century foreign journeys were only for the wealthy, and travel in Britain was restricted by poor roads. Stage coaches were not only uncomfortable and expensive, but often hazardous as well, and until the coming of railways the population was far more static than it is now. As a result only a few houses bore names of towns. Those that did usually had the name of a large town, a district or a county. In 1820 a Midlands town had some twenty-four properties so named. One was *Jersey Villa,* one was *Thanet Cottage,* two recalled spas—*Bath Cottage* and *Malvern House,* and the remainder were named after towns: *Nottingham House, York Cottage, Oxford Lodge,* or counties: *Rutland Lodge, Pembroke House* or *Dorset House.*

The Industrial Revolution not only brought a tremendous increase in urban populations, but changed the living conditions of thousands of people, and once the railways provided an easy means of escape from the grim atmosphere of industrial towns and cities, people began to travel as never before. Thomas Cook introduced his first excursion in 1841—Leicester to Loughborough for 1s, and others to Liverpool, Snowdonia and Scotland followed. But it was not until 1863 that the first tour to Switzerland took place, followed the next year by a tour to Italy.

Did this expansion of people's horizons influence their choice of house names in any way? A hundred years later it is impossible to question the householders concerned, and in many cases the houses themselves no longer exist, but houses began to have such names as *Italia, Gouray Villa, Jireh House.* In 1896 there was a *Roccabruna* in Bournemouth, a *Sorrento* in Paignton, and a *Cairo Lodge* in Weston-super-Mare. Whether because of the influence of Cook's tours or not, the use of foreign place names was on the increase.

However, although holidays with pay began to receive support at the turn of the century, many people lived in rented accommodation, much of which went unnamed, or else was named by the landlord and the tenants had to accept what was carved on the stone plaque in the gable.

By the 1930s both holidays and home ownership were on the increase, and this is reflected by the vast number of between-the-wars estates whose houses rejoice in *Tenby, Clevedon, Lymington, Lyme Regis, Colwyn, Harlech* or *Conway*. Few chose the seaside towns that attracted millions before World War II— Blackpool, Morecambe and Llandudno, preferring *Babbacombe, St Brelades, Lynton* or *Lynmouth*.

Not all holiday memories were of seaside towns; there were *Malham, Bala, Windermere, Borrowdale* and *Anglezarke*, which might at first be mistaken for a transferred place name from Scandinavia, but which is in fact a beauty spot on the Lancashire moors. As a house name it has appeared in Chester, Yorkshire and now Nottingham, since the owners concerned first chose it to remind them of pleasant hours spent walking in that area, and have taken the name with them when they moved house. An enrmous increase in travel has taken place since the end of World War II. Paid holidays are almost universal, and developments in air travel make it possible to reach all parts of Europe within a matter of hours, and the 'package' holiday has opened up the Continent to millions. Holiday horizons are widening to such an extent that as *Ilfracombe* and *Ambleside* had strong competition from *Rimini, Amalfi, Lugano, Ravenna, Cremona* and *Montserrat* a few years ago, there are now distinct signs of *Safari, Serengeti, Naivasha, Yellowstone, Thika* and *Kibigori*. *Samarkand* has already appeared, Bokhara and Tashkent are obvious further possibilities, but it is to be hoped that letter-writers and postmen will not have to struggle with Orjonikidzé and Piatigorsk.

HOLIDAY MEMORIES

From Britain	*From Elsewhere*
Aberdovey	Alicante
Afonwenn	Alsace
Anglesey	Aosta
Bettws-y-Coed	Benidorm
Bibury Cottage	Capri
Braemar	Como
Conway	Durban
Dovedale	Estartit
Gleneagles	Gibraltar
Ingleborough	Lloret de Mar
Kettlewell	Lugano
Kilve	Majorca
Llanberis	Nassau
Llandaff	Ostend
Llysfaen	Ravenna
Newquay	Rimini
Orkney House	Rome
Polperro	San Feliu
Ringwood	San Michele
Salcombe	San Remo
Sandown	Tahiti
Shetland	Tangier
Torbay	Valencia
Trossachs	Waikiki

CHAPTER 10

A Kind of Name Dropping

Can a house acquire prestige or atmosphere by borrowing a famous name? Many people evidently think so, and history, mythology, tradition, faraway places and the picturesque in general are eagerly ransacked. Great writers seem to have been aware of the way in which the name of a house can convey character and atmosphere—at all events authors are among the most formidable of name droppers.

Some names belong strictly to one house, and it might be overdoing it to borrow *Longleat* or *Castle Howard*, but seventy or eighty years ago the names of statesmen were in vogue and there were many houses called *Palmerston Villa, Beaconsfield House, Gladstone Cottage* and *Cornwallis*. Some members of the aristocracy were more popular than others, and Prince Albert had a number of cottages named after him. *Marlborough House* has always been a firm favourite. The Iron Duke was responsible for *Wellington Cottage* and *Wellesley Villa*. *Monson Villa*, a name used over a hundred years ago, probably commemorated Vice-Admiral Sir William Monson who, in his early naval career, was involved with the Spanish Armada and later was sent to raid the Spanish treasure fleet.

Some people prefer to give their houses a name with a general suggestion of blue blood—*Baronsmead, Earlswood* or *Knightwood*, and often these properties have been built on land originally owned by old, titled families. King and Queen both give rise to a large assortment—*Kingsmead, Kingscote, Queenswood, Queensway*; then there are *Dukes Meadow, Earldoms, Ladycroft, Ladybower* and *Ladywood*.

Scientists, writers, musicians, artists—all have lent their names —*Newton House, Hogarth, Jenner Lodge, Villa Dante, Haydn, Mozart, Ruskin Cottage, Herrick, Nash Cottage, Spengler House.* But all these are the great ones from the past, and it is very difficult indeed to find names on modern houses commemorating anyone born during this century. Perhaps this will come later on; more probably, the debunking of nineteenth-century hero-worship has done its work.

There are many fictional characters, too, from the past— *Hiawatha, Lorna Doone, Merlin, Rob Roy, Guinevere.* There is one neat transformation—Dr Watson's friend has been altered to *Sherlock's Holme.*

Apart from *Gemdene, Ruby Cottage* (named nearly a hundred years ago), *Topaz* and one of the most famous diamonds in the world, *Koh-i-Noor*, jewellery plays little part; *Double Diamond* refers neither to jewels nor drink, but has a diamond-shaped decorative stone in both its front gables, and similarly *Black Diamonds* has a diamond pattern in black in the brickwork.

Much preferred are links with early history—*Zenobia*, the ancient site in Syria; *Shiloh* in Jordan; *Petra*, the valley famous for its architectural remains; *Silbury*, the site of recent excavations in Britain, and *Serendip*, the early travellers' name for Ceylon. *Old Sarum* is popular. This was an ancient Celtic fortress and later a Roman fortress, and it is perhaps this that is implied and not the most notorious of the 'rotten boroughs' which had no houses at all within its limits when it was disfranchised in 1832.

Alhambra (more often associated in Britain with early music halls than houses) is nevertheless a reminder of the Moslem

97

G

fortress in Granada. The early invaders are not forgotten—
Vikings; *Saxons*; *Saracen Cottage*; *Mercia* after the Anglo-Saxon
kingdom founded in central England probably in the sixth century
and later to become one of the great earldoms until the Norman
Conquest, *Hengist,* the fifth-century warrior said to have been
Chief of the Jutes who, along with Horsa, founded the Kingdom
of Kent. One naturally expects, and finds, links with the Romans
—*Icknield* and *Fosseway,* both great Roman roads; *Chedworth*;
Eburacum and *Verulam* (now York and St Albans); *Chesters* and
Housteads, both after forts along Hadrian's wall. *Swan Street*
acquired its name solely because some 600 years ago it was the
first house to be built on the old Roman 'Swan Street'. Local
characters have been immortalised at *George's Plot, Tom's Acre,
Pickles Piece, Norton's Field* and *Giles Piece.*

The Cornish language offers some picturesque names: *Pen-
rose*—heath end; *Restronguet*—a ford by a tree-clad promontory;
Carminow—a very small enclosed space; *Chalcott*—a cow house
by a wood; *Chy-an-Dour*—a house by the water; *Chybean*—a
little house; *Langarth*—an enclosed space with a garden; *Caelean*
—legions' camp.

The Isle of Man has some splendid examples of delightful
names from the Manx language: *Thie Ain*—our house;
Loughen-E-Yeigh—pond of the geese; *Cronk My Chree*—hill of
my heart; *Creg Dy Shee*—rock of peace; *Cooil Veg*—little nook;
Garey Veg—little garden; *Reayrt Ny Howe*—view of the Howe,
a hillside village; *Yn-Cooill*—the nook; *Tarroo-Ushtey*—a
mythological water bull; *Keimagh*—a spirit said to haunt churchyard stiles; *Lhiannan-Shee*—a familiar spirit.

Myths and legends played a most important part in the lives of
people many centuries ago. They are part of the rich heritage of
children's stories and the basis of much that is most enduring in
literature. It is astonishing to find how many people have turned
to mythology in search of a house name, and one source in particular, the Arthurian legends, provides names all over the British
Isles. A great favourite is *Tintagel,* one of the legendary birth-

places of King Arthur and now a Cornish tourist attraction. *Camelot* is where King Arthur was said to have had his palace and court and where the Round Table was kept. Arthur himself evokes no interest at all, but his wife *Guinevere* and her lover *Lancelot* do. Sentenced to be burned, Guinevere was rescued by Lancelot, one of the most famous knights of the Round Table; she eventually became a nun and Lancelot a monk, but on her death she was allegedly buried with Arthur at *Glastonbury.* The two lovers and the town itself seem to have been commemorated, and the central character by-passed. But not so his magician, *Merlin,* who is supposed to have instituted the Round Table. He earns his place not only for the part he played at Court, but also for the story that, beguiled by an enchantress, he was left spell-bound in a bush and occasionally wakes to call out to the passer-by. (There is an even older legendary Merlin, a poet and prophet from the sixth century; *Merlin's Copse* is probably named after the bird, but the magician gives a much more romantic atmos-phere. The most frequently used name of all those concerned with King Arthur is *Avalon,* the Land of the Blessed, the Isle of Souls, an earthly paradise in the Western Seas. The great heroes such as Arthur and Ogier the Dane are supposed to have been carried there at death, and legendary figures hold court there.

Two more names continue the theme of death and the life beyond. *Valhalla,* the abode of Odin, was a warriors' paradise to which went only those slain in battle.

Whether the second example, *Elysium,* is a good choice or not rather depends where it has come from. In Greek mythology it referred to the banks of the river Oceanus where the blessed dwell. In Homer, the land has no snow, cold or rain and is in-habited by heroes who have been wafted there without dying. However, in Roman mythology the Elysian Fields were part of the underworld to which the Shades were sent. *Arcadia* and *Arcady* are distinctly more cheerful, being the ideal region of rural felicity.

Names of the gods themselves are often quite appropriate.

99

According to Roman legends, *Janus* was the two-faced god of beginnings, doorways and entrances, and was always invoked before all other gods in important undertakings. Some believe that doors (janua) were named for him, and some that he took his name from doors. *Mên*, god of the door, keeps watch and wards off evil spirits. He is one of five old Chinese gods who were supposed to preside in every household.

Zephyr comes from the god of the west wind, and *Aeolian House* from Aeolus, son of Hellen, founder of the people known as Aeolians, and god of the winds. The Aeneid describes how Aeolus kept the winds in a cave. Certainly these names make a change from the more usual *Windsmeet*, *West Winds* or *Four Winds* type of name.

Jupiter covers a great many household contingencies—god of thunder and lightning, guardian of law, protector of vineyards and the harvest, he regulated the course of human affairs and the name would therefore be one of good omen. *Hygeia* was the Greek goddess of health, later becoming the goddess of mental health.

Those interested in agriculture, or just plain gardening, have picked *Ceres*, the Italian goddess of grain and the harvest. Some choices appear to have no direct link with any building or household practices. *Medea*, wife of Jason, was a sorceress in Greek legends. She was one of the more turbulent immortals. *Undine* was a water sprite, and *Adonis* the beautiful young man loved by Aphrodite. *Minerva*, goddess of the artisans, seems a good choice. In Roman mythology she was the daughter of Jupiter, the supreme god, and one of the chief divinities. The first woman, *Pandora*, was created at the command of Zeus in revenge for the theft of fire from heaven. Forbidden to open the box she carried, she was finally overcome by temptation and out flew all the evils of life, with only Hope left behind. *Pan's Garden* suggests revelry; this ancient Arcadian god of flocks is often depicted dancing and playing the pipes.

Atlantis was a legendary isle in the Atlantic Ocean, whose

100

inhabitants reached a high degree of civilisation, but their land disappeared as the result of an earthquake. The popularity of the name undoubtedly comes from the idea of a mysterious ideal realm. And finally, *Parnassus*, a mountain in Greece sacred to Apollo, was the seat of poetry and music. All these names remind us of the prestige, in the old days, of a classical education.

Before the Industrial Revolution dwellings that went with jobs were frequently cottages, each belonging to a specific occupation—*Groom's Cottage, Reeve's Cottage, The Butler's Cottage, Weaver's Cottage, Potter's Cottage*.

Names of traditional skills and crafts still live on with the added attraction that they suggest an earlier more pastoral way of living—*Scrivener's Place, Stonepickers, Miller's Cottage, Forge Place*; and some have been adapted—*Woodman's Knap, Tyler's Crest, Yeomans, Keepersmount*.

One or two properties that were once business premises but are now private houses have still retained their original titles—*The Old Laundry, The Old Creamery, Old Granary, Old Cider Mill, Old Bank House, Old Malt House* and *The Old Gloving* are good examples. Some reveal that they were once pubs—*The Old Seven Stars, The Malt Shovel, The Old Dog, The Boot*.

But while it is often possible to base a name on an old occupation—*Cobbler's Knap* or *Shepherd's Hey* (also the name of Percy Grainger's most popular piano piece), present jobs create more of a problem. *Gasworks Cottage* and *Tramway Lodge* were functional names in the 1930s, and the Services have produced a few —*Admiral's Rest, Admiral's House, Major's Cottage, Sailor Cottage* and *Mariners*, with *The Commodore* for seaside guest houses. But strangely there are very few from the Royal Air Force: *Per Ardua*, from the RAF's motto, is about the only one, although *Biggin* might bring back memories of the Battle of Britain.

There are signs of the technological age in *Welder's Lodge* and *Quarks*. *Long Odds* was lucky for somebody, and *The Furs* is a

101

clever and intriguing variant on an old favourite. *Isomer* is a very interesting one, since the underlying characteristic of the chemical compounds it describes is of equal sharing.

Tramps Hall and *Beggars Roost* are romantic reminders of those who choose to wander the countryside, but it is known that one of the tramps concerned pursues the joys of the open road in his chauffeur-driven Mercedes.

An increasing number of people are being caught out by development, and while they were indeed *Back O'Beyond* or *Wayback* when they first moved in, they are now, more often than not, nothing of the kind. Half a century or more ago one *Boundary House* was accurately described, but today the borough extends at least a quarter of a mile beyond it. It is difficult enough to find addresses like *The Middle House, Nearby* or *Half Way Up,* but when *Omega* is nothing of the sort and *Top O' The Turn* and *Ways End* now adjoin yet another estate, it is even more puzzling. *The Other Cottage* is delightful when there really are only two, but *The House on the Left,* named more than forty years ago, had to acquire another name once the developers moved in. In entirely built up areas *Alpha* is still all right, but unless the plots are small, infilling could upset the sequence of *Beta, Gamma* and *Delta,* and at least one *Mono House* is now anything but alone. *The-Cottage-on-the-Common, The Cottage-in-the-Lane,* marvellous rural names; *Sally-in-the-Wood* and *Next-Door-to-Miranda*—splendid provided the people concerned remain where they are, but how much longer will it be before *Opposite the Ducks* and *Opposite the Cricketers Arms* and similar superb ingenuities follow the fate of *Turnpike House* and *Crossing Keeper's Cottage* and cease to be aids to navigation?

The old image of war as an occupation for gentlemen in which battles were splendid victories influenced names in the nineteenth century, but understandably less so after 1914. In the early part of the nineteenth century it was fashionable to call your house after one of the famous generals—*Buller House, Blucher Lodge,*

Wellington Cottage, Nelson Cottage, or after battles connected
with them—*Waterloo House, Trafalgar Cottage.* As the century
went by and one war gave way to yet another, even more grim
reminders appeared: *Ladysmith Cottage, Inkerman, Omdurman
House, Mafeking, Balaklava, Spion Kop, Malakoff* (a part of
metropolitan Paris, but also the hillside fortress in the Crimea,
besieged by the French and captured in 1855).

By the end of World War I there were fewer and fewer military
names being used; one or two like *Anzac* and *Zeppelin* were still
around in the 1930s, but since the last war the realities have been
too close for most people. Few houses were built while the war
was actually on, and people had more to do than to change their
house names to, say, Churchill or Eisenhower (although two narrow boats became *Montgomery* and *Wavell*). One family at least
had to do just the reverse and the house known as *Belsen* for
many years had to be changed.

There are now only a few names connected with World War
II, although even here there are possible reasons other than war
for the choice. *Normandy,* for example, is a popular holiday
area; *Falaise* (a name unaccountably popular), although the scene
of fierce fighting during the Normandy invasion in 1944, nevertheless has many other historical connections; it was the birthplace of William the Conqueror, and the scene of a number of
clashes between the French and the British in the fifteenth and
sixteenth centuries. Among other possible wartime names are
Troopers, Sappers and *Greenjackets.*

This does not mean to say that all references to war have disappeared entirely from our gateposts, but those that remain are
memories from history like *White Rose,* the emblem of the York-
ists, *Cromwell Cottage, King Charles Cottage, Boscobel,* and the
names of battles long since past, and the houses in question are
sometimes near the site where the battles took place—*Senlac,
Culloden, Naseby* and the last battle in England when the Royal-
ists overthrew the Duke of Monmouth—*Sedgemoor.*

Sport provides fewer names than might be expected. There

can be few people who are not aware of the impact of football, and yet of all the thousands of names seen, only *Scrummage* bears any reference to any of its forms. Golf is responsible for the most allusions—*The Links, Bunkers, Fairway, The Tees, Linksfield, Linksyde*; and a *Golf House* which was once a golf club. Most striking of all is the group of three houses vying with one another in the use of golfing names—*The Rough, The Cottage on the Green* and *The 11th Tee*. Cricket offers only *Cover Point* and *Bowling Over*. *Bowling Green House* carries a suggestion of immaculate turf, but houses called *Wimbledon* do not necessarily come into the same category as *Tennis Cottage*.

Perhaps *Two Litre Cottage* has a GT round the back, but in spite of all the advertising and the tremendous interest in cars, *Lagonda* is one of the few remembered. *Silverstone* has a champion, but not a Nurburgring in sight.

Fishermen are among the most prolific—*The Fishers, Fishers Croft, Shoal Waters, Casa de los Pescadores*: even the expression used by fishermen to wish each other good luck—*Tight Lines*. Sailing has a few—*Spinnaker, Sailcote, Black Sail, Slipways* and *Hove To. Checkmate* comes from chess. *Badminton* is the reverse process—a game named after a house, the Duke of Beaufort's home where it was first played in 1874.

Names of mountains are extremely popular, with a few such as *Kanchenjunga, Mont Blanc, Jungfrau, Parnassus* and *Everest* making frequent appearances. Perhaps some people feel that the acquisition of their own home is their personal equivalent of climbing the highest peak. And those who felt that only a volcano would do chose *Cotopaxi*, the highest active one in the world, though they have the excuse of the poem in which the names Chimborazo and Cotopaxi haunted the poet with their beauty.

In spite of the enormous popularity of recipe books and television series about cookery, food plays little part in house naming. The most amusing is *Quarter Cheese Cottage*, but the only others that seem to have remote connections with the larder are *Breadlands, Christmas Pie* (but not pudding) *House, Muffins, Pie Can* and *Jambalaya*—a dish of rice, prawns and ham. On reflection though, lard, bacon and macaroni are not quite as inspiring as the sources of *Afrormosia, Hacklebarney* or *Pantyquesta*.

Fruit and nuts exist almost by the ton. With apples and cherries well to the fore, the most favoured are native fruits, probably because many of the trees existed in the garden before the house was named. *Appleyard, Applecroft, Applegarth, Cherries, Cherrystone, Cherry Orchard*—there are innumerable variations, and other fruit like plums and pears too—*Plum Tree House* and *Pear Tree Cottage*. Two attractive and unusual names are *Chez Bilberry* and *Strawberry Tree House*, but while there are lots of *Vineyards* and *The Vines* the grapes they produce never seem to be included.

Mandarin seems to be becoming increasingly popular for what estate developers like to call 'superior detached residences', but this has other meanings beside fruit, such as a Chinese official or a colour. Otherwise oranges and lemons are few and far between, whereas there are several *Peach* and *Quince Cottages*.

The Nutshell, Nut Tree House, Walnut House, The Filberts, Almonds, Hazelnut Cottage, Chestnut Corner—apart from brazils and a few peanuts, there is a very adequate selection!

There is a limited range of fish—*Minnows, Sprat, Dolphin Cottage, Trout Hollow, Troutbeck, Shad Cottage,* and perhaps *Oyster Haven* could be included here. There is a *Shark House,* but this could lead to misunderstanding. Although there are relatively few fish names, a wrought iron fish skeleton is a popular decoration which can be seen alongside the name on the front of many houses. Wine lovers go for *Chablis, Martini, Barsac,* and *Sangria*. Someone in Portugal had the clever idea of naming two adjoining houses *Rosé* and *Branco*.

If there were a hit parade of house names, two musical examples would be strong contenders—*Greensleeves* and *Crimond*. Musical references tend to be classical, but this may yet change.

Today's pop fans are tomorrow's homeowners, in which case some pretty bizarre names are to be expected. While it seems quite acceptable to hang a sign outside saying *Ave Maria,* the day when someone lives in a *Yellow Submarine* is predictable. Just for the moment, though, it is *Mozart, Haydn* and *Faust Lodge,* with only a brief glimpse of *Donovan.* Although great names like Liszt and Beethoven are rare, *Cramer* has houses and streets named after him.

Music festivals and opera houses have some addicts—*Aldeburgh* and *Glyndebourne*—but not many. Terms like *Melody, Madrigal, Rhapsody, Octave House,* sometimes appear, and occasionally *Duet* and *Quintet* are used to denote the size of the family. But one of the most appropriate is *Portamento,* 'a gliding or passing from one pitch to another', which seemed to reflect the occupants' lives.

Although Gilbert and Sullivan are so popular, *Tit Willow* is one of the few representatives. Romantic links with the past are forged by reminders of favourite tunes like *Rose Marie, Tralee, Vienna Woods* and shows such as *Kismet* and *Carousel,* but the range of musical names is much narrower than might be expected in this century of radio and the gramophone.

With the growth of the reading public, it would have seemed logical to expect more literary associations than there actually are. Apart from *Pendennis,* Thackeray's novel published in 1850 which has provided hundreds of nameplates, Scott seems to have the greatest influence. *Ivanhoe,* which is world wide, heads the list, closely followed by *Waverley* and *Kenilworth,* with *Marmion* and its hero *Lochinvar,* and the Scottish outlaw *Rob Roy* behind.

Shakespearean names do not appear in the hordes one might have expected: there are *Elsinore, Cymbeline, Oberon, John O' Gaunt's* and *Cressida* in Britain, and a *Dunsinane* in Jamaica. *Northanger* and *Middlemarch* are less popular than *Cranford; Greenmantle* and *Lilliput* put in brief appearances and so do *Pookshill, Lodore* and *Stella Maris* (although at least one house of this name commemorates the ship that played such an important part in the relief of Malta during World War II).

Lear fans have come up with *Chankly Bore* and *Coromandel* (rather delightful for the kind of household it suggests), and those who chose *Toad Hall* and *Mole Cottage* had 'The Wind in the Willows' in mind.

Bleak House exerts a world wide fascination, but otherwise Dickens provides very little, apart from Mr Wardle's farm *Dingley Dell* which appears in several countries. *Ingoldsby,* from the series of satirical legends by R. H. Barham, has evoked considerable interest for many years, and a pre-war choice was *Gunga Din* (but this has now vanished); *Jorrocks,* R. S. Surtees' grocer, puts in the odd appearance, and there are a few *Utopias.* Two Scottish names closely connected with J. M. Barrie are *Thrums* and what is said to be its origin, *Kirriemuir,* but to the more ribald this latter name has acquired some rather different associations.

Alone from the world of pantomime is *Cinderella Cottage,* found both in England and Portugal; *Rubaiyat, Xanadu, Limberlost* and *Hobbits* have at least one mention each; there is a *Decameron* in Australia, and either T. S. Eliot's 'Four Quartets' or the name of the Somerset village led to *East Coker.* But whereas many names one might have expected to see are missing, others totally unexpected come to light, like *The Case Is Altered* from Ben Jonson's comedy produced in 1599. But apart from the use of a few authors' names such as *Dryden, Bronte House* and *Herrick* the list of names with literary associations is not very long.

As people turn to the most unlikely sources for inspiration—anything from war to witchcraft—one would have thought that there would be many more obvious direct links with the mass media than there are.

Daktari and *Tardis* probably fall into the television category, but one of the *Woodentops* is a timber construction and nothing to do with the delightful characters that amuse young viewers;

Panorama was in vogue before the documentary programme came into being. *Kildare* is the name of a US town. But probably the finest example is from a radio programme of some years ago, a house called *Much Binding* in Marsh, Bucks.

The names used by writers are well worth examining. One of the very earliest, somewhere between the eighth and tenth centuries, is given in Beowulf. It is related that Hrothgar, King of Denmark, built *Heorot* (also called *Hart*) *Hall*.

F. B. Pinion, in his book 'A Hardy Companion', explains that Thomas Hardy derived *Spaddleholt Farm* from the names of the villages of Chaddleworth and Sparsholt; *Knapwater House* was 'on a hill beside a lake'; the dairy farm he called *Talbothays* came from the name of the farm owned by Hardy's father; *Stancy Castle* is thought to have come either from the old Dunster family of Stanton or the neighbouring manor of Staunton. Two of the cottages had associations with birds—*Rook's Gate* and *Nest Cottage* (the home of Gabriel Oak), while *Rookington Park* is thought to have come from Heron Court. *The Slopes* was a modern house, but apart from *The Crags*, most of his houses had rather grand names—*Sherton Castle, Chateau Ringdale, Bramshurst Court, Corvsgate Castle, Chene Manor, Knollingwood Hall, Froom-Everard House, Enckworth Court* and *Stapleford Park*.

The world of Wodehouse's Catsmeat Potter Pirbright and Gussie Fink-Nottle revolves mainly round large stately homes with names like *Blandings Castle, Blicester Towers, Twing Hall, Matcham Scratchings, Smattering Hall* at Lower Smattering-on-the-Wissel; *Bleaching Court*. Apart from a few humble dwellings like *The Nasturtiums* in Jubilee Road, Wooster's friends inhabit vast mansions such as *Totleigh Towers* and *Ickenham Hall*, home of Pongo Twistleton's uncle. P. G. Wodehouse seemed to like names beginning with 'B'—*Biddleford Castle, Branstead Towers, Bumpleigh Hall, Brinkley Court* and *Binghampton Hall*.

Sherlock Holmes operated among the wealthy too, and many of his houses have imposing names—*Chiltern Grange, Yoxley*

Old Place, Manor Stoke House, Abbey Grange, Ridling Thorpe Manor, and *Appledore Towers.* For other houses he favoured 'gables' and we find *High Gable, Three Gables* and *The Gables,* and trees such as *The Cedars* and *The Copper Beeches.* Some of his houses had the more usual type of name such as *Fairbank* and *Briarbrae,* but there was one rare one—*Lafter Hall* in 'The Hound of the Baskervilles'.

Jalna, the house that figures so largely in Mazo de la Roche's 'Whiteoaks' series, was named after the military station in India where Adeline and Philip Whiteoak met and married. Readers of Dornford Yates will be familiar with his *White Ladies, Brooch,* and *Maintenance.* George Eliot's names merge convincingly with her landscape—in Silas Marner's village of Raveloe (itself used for a house in New South Wales), there was *The Red House* belonging to Squire Cass and Mr Osgood's *The Orchards.* Jane Austen chose *Netherfield House, Hartfield, Mansfield Park, Kellynch Hall* and *Whitwell.* The Bronte *Wildfell Hall* was most appropriate, and the *Fieldhead* in 'Shirley' was supposed to be *Oakwell Hall,* Batley.

Names which deliberately suggest atmosphere include *Nightmare Abbey, Dotheboys Hall, Castle Rackrent, Heartbreak House* and *Headlong Hall.* Melodramatic and sinister as these names may be, few can rival the chill with which any reader of Poe remembers a simple-sounding but ill-starred family name. One would not wish the most reckless of name-droppers to turn in at the drive and find.. . . .

'. . . the mighty walls rushing asunder—there was a long tumultuous sound like the voice of a thousand waters—and the deep and dank tarn at my feet closed suddenly and silently over the fragments of the *House of Usher.*'

A KIND OF NAME DROPPING

Avalon	Lords Piece
Beggars Haunt	Odd One
Boreas	Oddly Cottage
By-the-Mill	Oddtymes
By-the-Way	Old Needle House
By-the-Wood	Old Pump House
Camelot	Onaway
Crossbow	Opposite Three Poplars
Faraway	Other End
Forge Cottage	Over-the-Hill
Halfway Up	Over-the-Water
Hard to Find	Romans
Hideaway	Runnymede
Hundreds Apart	Starboard
Jura	The Bend
Kingsland	Tritons
Kingslea	Upalong
Knightscote	Up Over
	Ye Old Smithy

CHAPTER 11

Back to Nature

Whether you are in the middle of a city or in a remote country village, a walk round the houses will reveal the vast number of names with rural associations—trees, flowers, birds, animals, insects, the land itself, the elements, beauty spots—in fact anything that will bring reminders of the countryside.

In some cases, of course, *The Spinney* can actually be seen at the bottom of the garden, or there is a *Hill View* from the front windows, and perhaps *Meadowside* really is beside a meadow, but all too often names like *Greenfields* are only wishful thinking. Perhaps idealistic names can help in coming to terms with the necessity of turning former agricultural land into suburbia. If *Yonder Oaks* alleviates the sight of the nearby cooling towers, or *Honeysuckle Bower* helps to dispel the aroma of the vast chemical works, then why not? There are almost endless possibilities and permutations in the 'back-to-nature' theme.

In spite of the fact that the land and what lies beneath the soil is of vital importance in the building of a house, very few geological names are used. More than fifty years ago one house was called *Oolite*, and there are several with more familiar names like *Granite Villa*, *Flintstones*, *Chalkpit Piece*, *Clay Copse* and

Marle Cottage, but the main interest here lies in sand and stone, and stone is the more popular.

Many people seem to suffer from *Stoneacres, Stoney Woods, Stonyfields* and *Stoneydowns*; quite a few choose to live at *Stone House, The Stones* or *Stoney Paths*, and others at *Sandy Piece, Sandyhills, Sandy Nook, Sandfield, Sandy Gap*. One owner who was obviously delighted with his plot thought of *Joyous Earth*.

When land was more plentiful than it is today *Two Acres, Greenacres, Longacres, Cross-acres, Acremead* and the dozens of other ways of using 'acre' occurred quite frequently and appropriately, but *Acre End* is now perhaps more apt than *Crooked Acre* when it is being shared with ten other plots. Fields and meadows have provided inspiration for many names—*Fieldway, Fieldgate, Fieldside, Fallowfield, Midmeadow, Meadowside, Meadow Prospect*—but such names were far more possible some years ago, and there has been a tendency over more recent years to turn to names derived from the actual material used in construction: *Bricks* (with alternative spelling *Brix* and *Briques*); *Mortars*; *Pantiles*; tiles in various colours—*Greentiles, Bluetiles, Greytiles*; *Stonewalls*; *Timber Top*; *Old Stocks* (stocks being best-quality clamp-burnt bricks). Occasionally some architectural feature will be highlighted—*Cantilevers, Low Roof, Longeave, Chevron, Singlestack, Strawtop, Stairways, Tall Chimneys, Quoin, Dormer End*, but by far the most popular are gables in various forms—*Greygables, The Gables, Gable End* and *Gabledene*.

Azaleas to *Zinnias, Bluebells* to *Ylang Ylang* (a Malayan tree whose flowers are used to make perfume)—think of a flower and someone will have used it as a house name. *Forsythia, Foxgloves, Lavender Hill, Cowslip Ground, The Dahlias, Hollyhock House, Camelias, The Orchids, Rose Valley, Daisy Bank, Magnolia House, Jasmine Cottage, Cloverdale, Syringa Cottage*. An alternative version of the more familiar name is occasionally chosen: *Buddles* for marigolds; *Paigles* for cowslips. Sometimes the flower image is generalised: *Flower Patch, Petits Fleurs, Manyflowers, Fleurville, Spring Medley.*

Herbs have been used quite successfully for some names: *Mint Mead, Clove Cottage, Saffronfield, Saffron Platt, Mustard Copse, Nutmeg Cottage,* and pepper in different forms is surprisingly popular: *Peppers, Peppercorns,* and other forms such as *Peppermoss* and *Pepperstitch.*

From the wonderful variety of trees comes an abundance of names—*Oakwood, Oakdene, Oakmount*—an infinite variety all the way from *Acorns* to *Oak Tree House; The Alders, Larches, Beechwood, Two Chestnuts, Junipers, Cypresses, The Birches.* Firs provide the base for some attractive names—*Firbank, Firbeck, Fircones.* Pines grow well in some areas and lead to *Pinewood, Pinehurst, Pineneedles, Pinehangar* ('hangar'—a slope). Almost any tree can be turned into a name—*Cedarmead, The Limes, Hornbeams, Ashridge, Copper Beech, Silver Birch, Willow Vale, The Planes, Birch Hayes, Spruce Acres, Larchwind.* Trees are perhaps one of the biggest and most varied sources of names.

Although monkey puzzles are often found outside large, old houses yet *Monkey Firs* is one of the very few names using them. *The Laurels, Laureldene* and other names associated with laurels are to be found by the dozen among the older type of house. Over the years the laurel has come to symbolise victory and peace and is made into wreaths or crowns for the heads of champions, but it is also alleged to have magic power.

People with several different types of trees on their land sometimes choose more general names such as *Trees, Midtrees, Tall Trees, Twixtrees,* or even *Arboretum* (a tree garden). Near relatives are *Timbers, Timbertops,* or even *The Loggs.* Sometimes just parts of trees are used—*High Branches, Autumn Twiggs, Leaves* or *Conkers.* The word 'wood' has led to *Woodview, Woodfurlong, Woodneuk, Woodhangar, Woodways, By-the-Wood* and *In-the-Wood.* Quite the most frequently used, though, is *The Elms* and this name has been in vogue for at least

113

H

a hundred and fifty years, along with innumerable variants such as *Elmleigh, Lofty Elm, Elmside, Elm Beam, Barn Elms.* In the twelfth century, and perhaps even earlier, those guilty of crimes were 'by the heeles drawn thence to The Elmes in Smithfield and there hanged', and elms figure in myths from many parts of the world. Some thought an elm was the first woman; others that she was the mother of the goddess of fire; an elm growing in front of a Swedish home was regarded as the dwelling of the spirit who guarded the family. Whether people were aware of all these legends or not, well before *The Limes, Ashleigh* or *Oak Dene* figured on front doors, there was almost always an *Elm Cottage* or *The Elms* to be found in any group of named houses.

Those who have based their choice of name on the lawn—*Green Lawns, Lawnwood, The Lawns,* have committed themselves to spending endless time behind the mower. *The Grass Garden* or *Grasslands* is not so time consuming, and the scythe-it-once-a-year brigade have been realistic with *Wildacre* and *Nettles.* 'Garden' has been used in several different ways—*June Garden, Hortus* (Latin for garden), *Garden Cottage, Garden Walls, Garden Reach* and even *Garden of Eden.*

Although Britain is a nation of animal lovers domestic pets figure very seldom in house names. There are one or two dogs—*Beagles, Pekescroft* and *Poodleville,* but, with the exception of *The Cat House,* cats and kittens are remarkably few and far between.

With wild animals, however, particularly native ones, the case is different. One of the favourites is the badger, and it appears in a number of different forms, including *Badgers Hollow, Badgers Croft, Badgers Rake, Badgers Holt, Badgers Earth* and *Badgers Bend.* Even his nickname is used—*Brocks Sett* and *Brockhole.*

Closely following is the fox. Crafty, much hunted, it turns up time and time again: *Fox Run, Fox Dell, Fox Break, Fox Holes, Foxborough, Little Foxes, Vixens,* even *Reynard's Cottage.* Squirrels have a great following: *The Squirrels, Squirrel Run, Squirrels Leap, Squirrels Wood* and *Squirrel Bank.* Mice are

114

represented, despite women's reputed horror of them, in *Mouses Hollow, Mousehold House* and *Mousehole,* although this is also a Cornish village.

All kinds of animals come to light—deer: *Deer Hurst, White Fawn, Antlers, Deer Leap, Deerstalkers;* beavers: *Beavers Bank, Beaver Lee;* moles: *Moles Retreat, Mole End, Merriemoles;* rabbits and hares: *Warrenside, The Burrow, Coneybury, Haresway* and *Harehatch.* Less attractive ones—*Snakesfield, Bat's Cottage, Toad's Green.* Odd ones—*Lizard's Leap, Snail Creep, Horsehatches.* Very few sheep: *Lamb Cottage,* and a cow—*Vache View.* While hippos and rhinos are markedly scarce there are several reminders of the ox—*Oxleys, Oxpastures, Oxways,* and at least one each of *Panda, Kangaroo House* and *Bear House.*

But perhaps the problem has been solved once and for all by the people who have called their houses *Fauna* and *Noah's Ark.*

The popularity of bird names is of fairly recent origin. A hundred years ago many houses had names relating to trees and flowers, but birds were hardly mentioned at all. In the north, *The Rookery* and *The Eyrie* were among the very few from the world of ornithology. But all this has changed, and now birds feature in names all over the country. The British national bird—the robin —comes in a number of different forms: *Robindale, Robin Gay, Robin's Oak, Robin's Roost, Robin's Hey, Robin's Wood, Robin-a-Tiptoes* and, of course, *Robin Hill* of Forsyte Saga fame. Quite common, too, is the hawk: *Hawk House, Hawkhurst, Hawksdale, Hawkstone House, Hawksridge.* Other large birds have provided *Ravensgarth, Ravenshoe, Ravensmead, Eagles' Ledge, Eaglehurst, Eaglescroft.* The zoo as well as the neighbouring countryside provides examples: you are just as likely to see houses called *Flamingo, Penguins* or *Parrots* as you are to find *Sparrows' Thatch, Nightingale Cottage* or *Housemartins.*

The heron is seen all too infrequently, but it lends itself to some delightful names—*Heronwater, Herons Lake, Herongate,* and the superb *Potters Heron.* Owls are everywhere: *Owlpen, Owls Corner, Owlsmoor, Owlsleat,* and how about *Owl Hoot?* Larks somehow form very pleasant associations with high summer in *Larks Rise*, *Larkdown* and *Larkbarrow*. Then there are *Goose's Neck*, *Jays Hatch*, *Magpies* (by the dozen), *Swallow Tiles*, *Pigeon Point*, *Puffins*, *Cuckoo Corner* and *Cuckoo Bushes* (marvellous names for rural cottages); *Snowgoose*, *Plovers*, *Falcons*, and *Little Auk*. But the one seen most often is *Woodpeckers*, and occasionally its green variety—*Yaffles*. *Quail House*, *Pheasant's Rise*, *Swan Acre*, *Sandpipers* (or its alternative form *Tattlers*): there is no end to the variations, but those who couldn't make up their mind which bird to honour settled for *Warblers End*, *Birds Nest*, *Birdsong*, *Birds House* or *The Aviary*.

Naturally the weather provides a talking point. Hot countries encourage names like *Sun Valley*, *Sunshine House* or *Sunset Place*, while the names in cooler countries reflect more varied weather. All the winds—*North Wind*, *Southwind*, *East Winds*, *Westwinds* (*Fourwinds* and *Allwynds* cater for all contingencies, of course): *Windsmeet*, *Windwhistle*, *Windrise*, *Windspin*, *Windi Hi*, *Windward*, *Windleat*, *Downwind* (although here one wonders from what), *Boreas* (the North Wind) and the most original of all, *Snuff-the-Wind*. *Windcatch*, *Windswept*, *Wyld Winds* or *Crosswinds* suggest that sitting in the garden could be a chilly business, and *Hywinds* goes even further, but *Breezes* and *Little Clouds* are much more gentle.

Some people prefer to be reminded of specific winds, with *Chinook*, the warm dry wind in the Rocky Mountains, or *Mistral*, although this French wind would only serve to remind many of periods of frustration and bad temper. Others prefer *Gale Garth* and *High Force*.

Manyweathers is realistic, *Skyline* is noncommital, but although *Morning Calm* has a placid air it does raise suspicions about the previous night.

It is curious that so few names come from the rain; one or two raindrops or showers might have been expected; but *Storm House* and *Tempest Towers* have a positively Charlotte Bronte air. Mercifully fog seems to have been ignored; but snow has

116

produced the cheerful-sounding *Snowball Cottage, Snow Vale* and *Snowcott*.

Large, old houses frequently have *Sunnyside, Sunny Bank* or *Sunnydale* carved into the stonework by the gate, but although these names are found on modern houses 'sun' is used in a much wider variety of ways. Between the wars *Sunrays* was often accompanied by a sun-ray design on the gate or on a window of coloured glass; when picture windows came into fashion after World War II names like *Suntrap* spread, and now 'sun' appears in many different forms—*Sundawn, Sunward, Sunny Heights, Sun Oak, Sunpatch*.

Perhaps the exploration of outer space will lead to a whole crop of new names: at the moment *Moonrakers* easily leads *Moonhill, Half Moon* or *Moonsgreen. Hunters Moon* is the next full moon to the harvest moon; *Moonfleet* is very topical, and *Moonacre*, chosen for an entirely different reason, may well turn out to be prophetic. Long before exploration of space, house owners had borrowed from the night sky: *Jupiter, Cassiopeia*, and *Aquila*, the constellation in the Milky Way said to have the outline of an eagle carrying away Antinous, boy page to the Emperor Hadrian.

Morning, noon and night—they appear on gateposts almost as regularly as they occur each day: *Morningside, Dayspring, Daydawn*, followed by *High Noon*, and finally *Eventide, Sundown, Dusk* and *Evening Hill*. Somehow the afternoon gets left out, but perhaps this is where *Forty Winks* and *Siesta* come in. All four seasons are remembered: *Springtime, Springhaven, Summer Orchard* and *Summer Ley, Autumn Tints* and *Autumn Twigs*, and there are plenty for winter—such as *Winterset, Winterhill, Winterbrook* and *Winterslow*.

Although *Christmas* is sometimes used for cottages and *Christmas Pie* for one house, the months of December and November have little appeal: much preferred are *January* (and sometimes *Janvier*) *Cottage, April Cottage, June Cottage, May Villa, Septembers* or *October House*. Apart from Christmas, other feasts

117

and festivals give us *Michaelmas Croft, Lammas Cottage,* *Candlemas Cottage, Midsummer Cottage,* and *Fiesta.* It is strange that the only day of the week so far encountered is *Friday Cottage.*

Local beauty spots have provided some excellent names. In the Cotswolds there are dozens of houses named *Windrush*; the North abounds in 'dales' of one kind or another—*Swaledale, Dale House, Dale Garth, Grassendale, Nidderdale, Wharfedale House*; the Downs have endless combinations—*Downside, Downhurst, Downleaze*; Cannock Chase offers *Chase View, Chaseside* and *The Chase.* Of course, names are often transferred and many a *Windermere* or *Ambleside* can be seen in the south, with *Snowdon* or *Ben Nevis* rearing their heads in the most unlikely places. Rivers are another good source, with *Derwent* one of the favourites, and many others like *Thames View, Cherwell House; Trent Villa, Tynedale, Tweed, Severnside* or *Ribble Bank.*

You do not have to be a guest house proprietor in order to call your house *Sea Vista* or *Ocean View.* The *Seaview* type of name has been widely adopted all round the coast. Here, of course, finding a name is no problem, since there is a ready-made source on the doorstep—*Sea Crest, Sea Winds, Sea Whispers, Sea Knoll, Seawaye, Seacot. Seascape* gives the feeling of wide open spaces, so do *Atlantic View* and *Ocean Glory.* There is no shortage of suitable names even if you are not actually living on the promenade: *Gulls Cry, Gullsway, Seagulls, Harbour Lights, Mariners, Middle Watch, Sealight, Sea Holly*—all of these have a distinctly coastal air about them.

Modern smuggling is all too frequently connected with unglamorous customs sheds, but there are any number of reminders of the past in *Smugglers Cottage* or *Smugglers Ride. Robbers Roost* sounds intriguing and whatever happened at *Smugglers Leap*?

Some of the most attractive names are given to cottages. 'Cottage' (meaning village dwelling or small country residence) or its shortened form 'cot' appear in innumerable combinations, such as *Oak Tree Cottage, Dovecot, Cobweb Cottage, Trout Cottage*. What we visualise here, of course, is the one- or two-storied thatched dwelling with tiny windows, genuine old beams, and a garden ablaze with flowers. Just occasionally a ten-bedroomed mansion with carriage lamps to light its drive will try to persuade us that it is *Gnomes Cottage*.

Basket Cottage, Candlemas Cottage, Dawn Cottage, Moth Cottage, Quince Cottage. Where else would you find such romantic ones as *Anniversary Cottage, Kiss Cottage*, or *Romany Cottage*? And all the flowers—*Snowdrop Cottage; Lilac Cottage, Daffodil Cottage, Jasmine Cottage, Orchid Cottage, Clematis Cottage, Periwinkle Cottage, Lavender Cottage, Violet Bank Cottage*. Then the birds—like *Nightingale Cottage, Owl Cottage* and *Cuckoo Cottage*. And for sheer realism—*Sheepwash Cottage* and *No Oven Cottage*. Intriguing names like *Stonepickers Cottage* (were they roadmenders or geologists?); happy names like *Jumble Cottage, Dancing Green Cottage* and *Melody Cottage*; names with religious overtones—*Pilgrim Cottage* and *Pulpit Cottage*; all kinds of names—*Saucy Cottage, Cream Pot Cottage, Mop Cottage, Lace Cottage, Pencil Cottage, Pillar Box Cottage, Cara Mia Cottage*—Britain is probably unique in the variety of its cottage names.

BACK TO NATURE

Birds Nest
Boarfield
Bowindow
Bluebell Corner
Calf View
Candletrees
Candy Cottage
Catkin Cottage
Copper Top
Crabtreebeck
Deerstalkers
Doubledoors
Flat Roofed House
Flue Winds
Fossil Cottage
Grassgarth
High Stile
Honeybee Cottage
Hop Blossom Cottage
Larksgaye
Little Frogs
Magpies
Moonville
Moth Cottage
Nettles

Old Well House
Owls Barn
Queerwinds
Rogues Roost
Sea Haze
Shrubbery
Smallpiece
Smallstones
Snail Creep
Stonewalls
Stonewold
Strawtop
Sundial Cottage
Tattletrees
Tawny Barn
The Ark
The Burrow
The Leaves
Thickets
Thistledown
Thistles
Tulip Tree House
Twa Lums
Verbena
Wheatfield
Wynd-y-Nook

CHAPTER 12

Triumph and Disaster

Some people obviously go to a great deal of trouble to find suitable and often quite delightful names for their houses. There are, for example, *Tadpole House* in Frog Lane, the Cheese family who live at *The Mousetrap*, Mr and Mrs Wall and their two daughters who named their house *Four Walls*, and *Pan Yan* on Pickler's Hill. The Dickens enthusiasts who found themselves living in Copperfield Road took full advantage of this and called their residence *Micawber House*; the lucky recipient of *Walter's Gift* knew how to show appreciation. Were the owners of *Barley Picle* paying tribute to one of the first cereals cultivated by man? What moments of inspiration produced *Zen-in-the-Wood*, *Friday's End* or *Pogies*? One would very much like to know who *Gentle Jane* was. The name has the simplicity of a folk tune. The level of wit and imagination among house names is very high, and many who might never have considered themselves poets have achieved a poetry of their own in names like *Smockfarthings* and *Next-door-to-Miranda*.

It is only natural that where there is poetry there should also be rhetoric and the occasional disaster.

Some names at first sight appear to come from a foreign

language, but further investigation reveals that they are nothing more than names turned backwards; *Nostaw, Notwen, Evilo, Revilo, Rood Egats*—here perhaps they are following in the footsteps of Dylan Thomas's Welsh village of Llareggub.

Another way of using a surname is to add an ending such as 'croft' or 'land': the Foxes at *Foxcroft*, the Brookes at *Brookland*, the Scotts at *Scotland*. Occasionally, but this is more difficult to achieve, a palindrome turns up: in 1929, for instance, there was a *Noyon*.

Deliberate misspellings—*Chez Wen, Winderview, Nuhaven, Kosikot*; spoonerisms—*Gorldy Woods* for Worldly Goods—numbers made into names like *Fortitoo*; manufactured words from phrases like *Idunno*; puns such as *Shilly Chalet*—all these are popular devices which explode in the path of the unwary. Sometimes the search for a distinctive identification is almost too successful.

The funny-ha-ha namers are perhaps those who are most certain to regret their moments of sudden enthusiasm. A house is still a fairly permanent object, likely to endure while much around it changes.

Tiz Yer, Gnuwun, Y Wurree, The Last Straw, At Last (or if you want to go one further, *En Fin*), *Oddspot, Muchado, Whipas, Gone to Ground, Why Not, Eureka*—all very funny at first. But to see gates bearing such legends (usually in Gothic type) as *Paide, Keen-Uns, Sudden-Lee, Lylo, Socosi, Linga Longa* is to feel slightly uncomfortable. Will the occupants greet the visitor with sneezing powder or clockwork mice? Jokes that have to be explained are even more trying; *Snicere* (from 'It's nice here') rather lost its point when the local inhabitants insisted on pronouncing it 'Snickery'. Pride of ownership is only natural, particularly in one's first house, but in names like *Owzitiz, Hisn' Hers, Ersanmyne*, it is possible to feel that pride has gone before a fall.

When houses were scarce names like *Hunt's End, Found, Stumbledon, Tether's End, Witsend, Fairly Hunted*, might have sounded like a cry of triumph, but some of them may be read as a double-edged compliment suggesting the house was the best of a bad bunch.

The task of the estate agent is not likely to be made easier by *Swamps Edge, Mire House, Malmains, Bog Bottom* or *Dampach*. In your search for a home would you be anxious to go and see *Roughit, The Shack, The Shanty, Rusty Railings, The Hutch, The Huddle* or *Loafer's Glory?* Most surveyors would look twice at the fabric of *Crumbledown* or *Crumbleholme*. What lies in store for you at *Crazydale* or *Nutter's Nest? Duffers, Nuts* or *Allnuts* gives fair warning. On the other hand, does *Neat Home* appeal? Perhaps *Paradise* or *The Garden of Eden* is going a bit too far the other way.

Crime has become a way of life, but it is doubtful whether this was in the minds of the proud owners who named their houses *Holloway, Newgate* and *Brixton*. The MP who lived in *Borstal Tower* in 1790 would have had second thoughts today. Although houses called *Botany Bay* doubtless commemorate the place where Captain Cook made the first landing in Australia in 1770, historically its name has long been connected with the penal colony which once existed there on the site of what is now Sydney.

Red Roke probably conveys to its owners a meaning quite different from that found in the dictionary, where 'roke' means smoke, steam, vapour, mist, fog or drizzling rain!

Anything to do with rats like *Rats Cottage* or *Rats Castle* usually gives people the shudders. And who wants to be reminded of *Hangovers?*

There is nothing new in the idea of naming a house after the christian name of one of its occupants, and even in the early nineteenth century you could find *Georgina House* or *Mona Cottage*, but it was not particularly fashionable. Of course, at that time many of the houses with names belonged to 'the gentry', and thus the forenames tended to be of the rather grand variety:

Georgiana Villa, Winifred House, Aubrey Lodge, Rollo Cottage
or *Julian Villa.*

As the years went by, more and more christian names crept in,
often with 'ville' tacked on the end—*Maryville,* and *Lauraville.*
The fashion in personal names is reflected in house names, and
around the turn of this century when house names were increasing there were many like *Ethelville, Eva Villa* and *Florence
House,* and although girls' names have always been used more
often than boys', there was the occasional *Herbert Villa* or
Normanhurst. By the 1930s there were dozens: *Gertiville,
Alexandra Cottage, Algernon House, Edith Lodge, Alfred House.*
Then came a custom which is perhaps more fashionable today
than ever before—that of inventing a house name from the joint
names of the owners, and as some people tattoo the names of their
nearest and dearest in intertwined forms over various parts of
their anatomy, others intertwine them on the front door.

Ronald, married to Doreen, lives at *Rondor,* and at *Valtone*
live Valerie and Tony; Muriel and Stanley are at *Muristan,* and
Kenneth and Patricia at *Kentricia;* Sheila and Martin have *Sheil-
mar,* while Marion and Arthur live at *Maranartha.* This method
is useful if your name is Donald—*Joydon, Brendon, Syldon,
Rosedon,* or John, shortened to 'jon' at *Penjon* and *Marjon.*

The possibilities are endless: *Dy-Anjo, Georjan, Robella,
Ronruth, Algwen, Sidnel, Bernivy, Eljym, Bel-les, Franmarg,
Kerstan, Davejoy, Evenlen, Sidella, Deneve, Walmar, Monteve,
Wilwyn, Fremar, Idaron, Ivandor, Cymar, Robeth, Trevera,
Kathbri, Lydnor, Jacris, Kenwyn,* even *Darlin* and *Shapaudra*
(a combination of Sharon, Pat, Paul and Sandra).

It is not, of course, necessary to stick merely to christian names
—two surnames can often be just as easily linked. Mary Williams
married to Frank Martin had the choice of *Wilmar* or *Martiams.*
Sometimes initials instead of names are used: *The Jais, Jaybee,
T-an-M,* and less fortunately, *Emange;* or else one name plus
suitable ending: *Willsdene, Bryansgate, Basildene, Louisville,*

Maesholme, Benmead. Dwand stands for 'dry, warm and no draughts', and *Myob* for 'mind your own business'.

A certain amount of disharmony is suggested by some names—for instance *Quarrels Copse, Gossips, Quandry,* or *Loggerheads* (although those with a good knowledge of Midland geography would know this is also a place name).

But how long will the postman go on calling, or friends go on writing, if you name your house *Nkokonjeru, Scheherazade* or *Buakonikani?* Even the simplest names can be misspelt, let alone *Casa de loss Pescadores, Slieve-Na-Mon, Nos-Y-V'la, Steenwijk, Ceale Mine* or *Shak Aizle.* There is an unmistakably sickly glow, as from one of those television lamps in which the liquid moves up and down, about *Our Nest (Le Nid* if you must), *Wee Hame* or *Snugboro.* After such names it is a satisfying antidote to move on, with incredulous delight, to *Cobblers.*

Certain names chosen with the best of intentions have now come into the 'unfortunate' category, since fashion changes, new words appear in the language, or slang words take on different meanings. A good example of this is the word 'loo' which has crept into everyday usage over the past fifteen years, and led to one man calling his house *Lautrec* because he had two loos. No doubt endless embarrassment is now caused to the owners of houses called *In The Lew* (in spite of the fact that the word 'lew' is a dialect one dating back at least 350 years and meaning 'sheltered from the wind; warm and sunny'), *Toulouse, Inverlooe.* It is sad, but not surprising, that a house once called *Hetts Loo* now bears an entirely different name. *Allmodcons,* on the other hand, is clearly intentional.

Regional usages can too sometimes lead to rather unfortunate choices—*Upyonda* refers to the position of a house on a hillside; it is one of those quirks that in some parts it is the euphemism for cemetery. *Bra-Cove* was named before such garments had been invented; small wonder the house now merely bears a number. *Little Onn* is named after a Midlands village, but its occupants must long ago have wearied of jokes about non-stop

125

revue. Similarly, to choose *Lime House* is rather asking for quips about Chinese laundries or chop suey. Your diestamped notepaper may be of the highest quality, but will the impression be sustained if you call your house *Clochemerle*? And what does *Casanova* do for the man-about-the-house?

There are always some names that appear to come from unusual objects, or for reasons that are not immediately apparent. *Truckles*—'truckle' being a low bed, at one time particularly used by servants; *Tweakers*—a tweak is a sharp wringing pull or twitch; *Diggins*—the only conclusion that can be drawn here is that it must be a corruption of 'diggings' meaning lodgings; *Grubbins*—this may, of course, be pure invention on the part of the owners, as the nearest proper word is the verb 'to grub', to dig superficially, or to uproot; and *Beanto* leaves one wondering just where to. *Bodgers* could be the home of honest, enthusiastic, but perhaps not very expert do-it-yourselfers, since the other meaning refers to pedlars. Although *Clinkers* may suggest the remains of a dead fire, they can be very hard bricks, pale in colour, made in Holland and used for paving. *Hickbibby*, a farm near Wigan, is from the Latin 'hic bibi' (here I drink). *Ladsani* rather neatly records the fact that the house was built and lived in by a father and his two sons.

If you move house frequently then *Trotters* would not be quite as outrageous as it may at first sound, for although trotters conjures up pigs' feet they can also refer to people who move about briskly and constantly. And what about *Little Grunters, The Troggs, Clamerkin, Tumblers, Upender, Clamber, Trespassers W—*?

> Is there anybody there? said the Traveller
> Knocking on the moonlit door

The inscriptions on some moonlit doors would be more than enough for Mr de la Mare himself.

In the lead are the pixies—*Pixies Nest, Pixies Haunt, Pixies Dell, Pixies Halt, Pixies Mead, Pixies Holt,* and then there are

Goblins, Goblins Glade, The Elf, Elflands, Gnomes Cottage, Dwarf Cottage and the *Little Folks* themselves. *The Hoppit, Twinkles, Gladnest, Fokia, Chix, The Crib, Puck's Oak, Pan's Garden, Tweeney Cottage,* and *Bunny's Leap.*

Travellers, whether de la Mare's or others, should be warned that certain parts of the country may be approached only with an emergency kit including the works of Samuel Hoffenstein, particularly the following:

> Then out of the forest Grandfather Nightmare
> Rides in a chariot of Stilton cheese
> And eats the ninnies, the oafs and the zanies
> The rabbits, the elves and the walnut trees.

TRIUMPHS AND DISASTERS

Astir Cottage
Barn Platt
Barley Picle
Bonanza
Bunny's Leap
Bunyeroo
Cobblers Meadle
Coromandel
Ethelburt
Fiddlers Elbow
Fiveleaps
Found
Gauntlets
Gertieville
Gnuwun
Grace Dieu
Grandfathers
Granneys
Hacklebarney
Kon Tiki
Larkbarrow
Lautrec
Lazybed
Little Grunters
Nayles

Nitkins
Nittings
Nu-Holme
Pipers Patch
Pixies Nest
Pogies
Pookshill
Quando
Quintillion
Robann
Rojamin
Samandor
Smockfarthings
Sumware
Tankards
The Humpy
The Shambles
Traynes
Tumbledown House
Tweeney Cottage
Utopia
Vereroy
Wee Hoose
Whynot
Yaffles Haunt

CHAPTER 13

End-of-the-Street

A look at the names in almost any road is unexpectedly revealing and suggests several lines of thought.

How do we resemble or differ from our ancestors? We are beginning to know what people ate and wore, how they hunted and fought, what pictures they made of the gods they worshipped. But how did they describe their homes? How far back do the jokes and the imagery begin? How important was the right name in keeping out hostile tribes or evil spirits? There must undoubtedly have been some fine names which are now lost to us.

It is difficult to draw any conclusions about the distribution of particular names, or types of names between one locality and another. There are differences of style and period, possibly even hints of class differences: naming has its gradations from the seaside-holiday-whelk-stall and postcard jollity at one extreme (*Tiz-Yer* and *Y-Wurre*) to a level of social and verbal sophistication (*Isomer*) which suggests that architect and landscape gardener have not laboured in vain. Given a certain list of names (*Wayneflete, Coombe Lodge, Ashanti, Menton, Carlyle House*) one can almost picture the road. It also seems that different aspects of the habit can be catching: it is very noticeable that one road will show a sequence of uniformly banal and uninspired names, while a similar stretch of road less than half a mile away will produce a succession of fresh and inventive names, as if the first arrivals had set the tone, and their neighbours had been inspired to follow on.

Fashions change. In present-day England 'villa' and 'lodge' would not be among the popular choices as new names, whereas 'casa' 'finca' 'villa' 'vivenda' and 'maison' are still in vogue in Europe. There are fashions too in house name plates. A current choice is the slice of rustic timber, protected with a coat of polyurethane gloss, and with the name usually in black; Gothic type seems to be regaining popularity. Newer still are simple black letters on a luminous silver-coloured background, each letter set in a separate rectangle. Names carved in stone are now too expensive and too permanent to be widely popular. (The difficulty of climbing up and removing the work of past stonemasons continues to preserve some invaluable things for us). In Europe wrought-iron longhand has been fashionable for some years, and examples of black-enamelled schoolgirl script are now beginning to writhe up the fronts of English houses.

Throughout the English-speaking world there is a great interchange of names, brought about by travel, service in foreign parts, and the many ties of tradition and circumstance that bind families and countries together. Particularly notable are the popularity of Australian and Indian names all over England, and the 'more English than the English' names still to be found on many houses in India and Pakistan.

Although names like *Mon Repos, Chez Nous* and *Dunrovin* have long since been regarded as jokes, yet they still appear throughout the world. *Wychwood*, surprisingly, is the favourite that turns up everywhere; in Britain some of the commonest names are *The Spinney, Avalon* (also found on the Continent), *Greensleeves* and *Crimond*.

Colours rank high, with white, blue and green particularly

popular. There must be thousands of *White Houses*, even though some of them are painted yellow; and a miscellany of objects come in blue and green—*Blue Hills, Blue Cedar, Blue Field, Greenacres, Green Bushes, Greendrift, Green Haze* and *Green Tiles*.

Other perennials are *Lanterns, Tanglewood, Cherry Orchard, Wayside, Woodpeckers*; references to trees: *Treetops, Three Trees, Tree View, Tall Trees*; innumerable varieties of gables: *Grey Gables, Gable End, Gabledene, Gablecroft*; and anything that can be tacked on to high—be it *High Fences, High Noon, High Raise, High Standing, High Hoe* or just *High Hopes*.

In earlier times religion and the family name, identification and possibly pride of ownership seem to have had the emphasis. But as we approach modern times the element of personal expression, as distinct from simple identification, gains importance. What might once have been a family motto, a war cry or an heraldic device is now a shout of defiance from the front gate.

Not only the element of expression but also the range of references—to literature, mythology, music, folklore and contemporary events—seems to be widening. And in spite of difficulties of spelling (and frequent mistakes) names from other languages and countries grow in popularity: Manx, Aboriginal, Maori, Cornish, as well as the major European languages are widely drawn upon.

Just as people are more uninhibited than one expects, so are they also much more ingenious, imaginative and original. If the original owners of *The Vyne, The Seven Deadly Sinnes, Megses Glorie* and *Bachelor's Tower* could revisit us today, they would surely be proud of their successors.

Bibliography

Andersen, Johannes C. *Old Christchurch*. 1949

Australian Council of National Trusts. *Historic Homesteads of Australia*. 1969.

Baker, Agnes C. *Historic Abingdon*. 1963

Baker, Agnes C. *Historic Streets of Abingdon*. 1957

Barnhart, C. L. (Ed). *New Century Cyclopedia of Names*. 1954

Bartholomew, J. G. *Literary and Historical Atlas of Europe*. 1915-17

Benedictine Monks of St Augustine's Abbey, Ramsgate. *The Book of Saints*. 1966

Binani, G. D. and Rama Rao, T. V. *India At A Glance*. 1953

Briggs, Asa (Ed). *The Nineteenth Century : the Contradictions of Progress*. 1970

Carcopino, Jerome. *Daily Life in Ancient Rome*. 1941

Cook, Thomas & Son Ltd. *The Story of Thomas Cook*

Copley, G. J. *English Place Names and Their Origins*. 1968

Dexter, T. F. G. *Cornish Names*. 1968

Elder, J. R. *Glimpses of Old New Zealand*. 1924

Folsom, Merrill. *Great American Mansions*. 1963

Fodor's *Guide to India*. 1967

—. *Guide to The Caribbean, The Bahamas and Bermuda.* 1968
Friedländer, Ludwig. *Roman Life and Manners,* 2. 1908
Funk and Wagnalls. *Standard Dictionary of Folklore, Mythology and Legend,* edited by Maria Leach. 1949
Hardingham, John. *New Zealand Travel Guide.* 1959
Hardwick, Michael and Mollie. *The Sherlock Holmes Companion.* 1962
Harris, John. *Buckingham Palace.* 1968
Historic Houses, Castles and Gardens in Great Britain and Ireland. 1969
Hole, Christine. *Witchcraft in England.* 1945
India Who's Who. 1969
Jaggard, Geoffrey. *Wooster's World.* 1967
Jervis, J. and Kelly, V. (Eds). *The History of Woollahra*
Kingsford, C. L. (introduced by). *Stow's Survey of London 1603.* 1908
Lawson Dick, Oliver (Ed). *Aubrey's Brief Lives.* 1968
Lea, J. *A New Guide to Cheltenham and Its Environs.* 1837
Luckenbill, Daniel David. *The Annals of Sennacherib*
McWhirter, Norris and Ross. *The Guinness Book of Records.* 1970
Michelin. *Switzerland.* 1969
Moreau, S. *A Journey to Cheltenham Spa.* 1786
Morris, James. *Venice.* 1960
Muirhead, L. Russell (Ed). *The Blue Guides—Belgium and Luxembourg.* 1963
—. *The Blue Guides—Switzerland.* 1948
Nagel's *Encyclopaedia Guide, Bulgaria.* 1968
—. *Guide Books, Belgium and Luxembourg.* 1950
Nicholson, Nigel. *Great Houses.* 1968
Petersen, G. C. *Who's Who in New Zealand.* 1968
Pinion, F. B. *A Hardy Companion.* 1968
Posener, G. *A Dictionary of Egyptian Civilisation.* 1962
Rivet, A. L. F. 'The British Section of the Antonine Itinerary', *Britannia 1.* 1970

133

Ruff. *Beauties of Cheltenham*. 1806

Salter, H. E. *The Historic Names of the Streets and Lanes of Oxford*. 1921

—. *Map of Medieval Oxford*. 1934

—. *Properties of the City of Oxford*. 1926

Saunders, David (Ed). *Historic Buildings of Victoria*. 1966

Sawyer, P. H. *The Place Names of the Domesday Manuscripts*. 1956

Sharpe, R. R. (Ed). *A Calendar of Wills in the Court of Hustings*. 1889

Sprigge, Sylvia. *The Lagoon of Venice*. 1961

Stuart Jones, H. *Companion to Roman History*. 1912

Swan, Michael. *British Guiana*. 1957

Townsend, J. *News of a Country Town*. 1914

Turner, Reginald. *The Smaller English House*. 1952

White, Osmar. *Guide to Australia*. 1968

Who's Who of Southern Africa. 1970

Wood, Margaret. *The English Medieval House*. 1965

Acknowledgements

I am grateful to all those people who have helped in various ways with the making of this book. Particular thanks are due to Mr C. V. Crellin of Peel, Isle of Man; Mr R. J. Hutchings, Manager and Curator, British Waterways Museum; Mr Angus Thomson, Press Officer, George Wimpey & Co Ltd; Mr P. Brightmore; Mrs V. I. Miles; the Records Department, Central Headquarters, the Post Office; the Superintending Architect of Metropolitan Building (Greater London Council); the Housing Manager, Manchester Corporation; the Librarians of the public libraries of Abingdon, Birmingham, Blackpool, Brighton, Dudley, Cheltenham and Oxford, and of the Bodleian Library; the staff of Australia House, New Zealand House, South African Airways, and the Embassies and travel offices of Holland, Belgium, Italy and West Germany.

Acknowledgements are also due to Livright Publishers, New York for permission to quote the extract from the parody 'Mr de la Mare makes the Little Ones Dizzy' from 'A Treasury of Humorous Verse' by Samuel Hoffenstein, and to Chatto & Windus for permission to quote the lines from the poem 'Let it Go' from the Collected Poems of William Empson.

Finally I thank most sincerely all those other friends who have helped the progress of this book in innumerable ways.